ALL YOU REALLY NEED TO KNOW
ABOUT PRAYER
YOU CAN LEARN FROM THE POOR

ALL YOU REALLY
NEED TO KNOW
ABOUT
Prayer
YOU CAN LEARN
FROM THE POOR

LOUISE PERROTTA

Foreword by
FERDINAND G. MAHFOOD

Photography by
GINA FONTANA

CHARIS

SERVANT PUBLICATIONS
ANN ARBOR, MICHIGAN

Charis Books is an imprint of Servant Publications especially designed to serve Roman Catholics.

Most Scripture references are from the New Revised Standard Version of the Bible, © 1989 by the Division of Christian Education of the National Council of Churches of Christ in the USA. Used by permission. All rights reserved. Passages from the Psalms have been taken from *The Psalms, Singing Version* © 1963 by The Grail and reprinted by Fount Paperbacks in 1977. All rights reserved. Psalm numbers and verses may vary according to the versions used. Psalm and verse numbering in this book correspond to the NRSV.

Published by Servant Publications
P.O. Box 8617
Ann Arbor, Michigan 48107

Interior Photos: Gina Fontana
Cover Photo: © W. Cody/Westlight. Used by permission

96 97 98 99 00 10 9 8 7 6 5 4 3 2 1

Printed in the United States of America
ISBN 1-56955-028-X

LIBRARY OF CONGRESS CATALOGING-IN-PUBLICATION DATA

Perrotta, Louise
    All you really need to know about prayer, you can learn from the poor / Louise Perrotta.
        p.   cm.
    ISBN 1-56955-028-X
    1. Church work with the poor—Catholic Church.   2. Church work with the poor—Caribbean Area.   3. Catholic Church—Caribbean Area—History—20th century.   4. Spiritual life—Catholic Church.   5. Prayer—Catholic Church.   6. Caribbean Area—Church history—20th century.   I. Title.
BX1448.P47   1996
277.29'0829—dc20   96-46519
                                                                              CIP

CONTENTS

A powerful conversion during a 1976 plane trip gradually changed Ferdinand Mahfood from a high-powered businessman to a high-powered "beggar for the poor." Improving the lives of people like these playful girls at a Haitian orphanage is the aim of Food For The Poor, the relief organization Ferdy founded in 1982.

FOREWORD

ALL I'VE REALLY NEEDED TO KNOW ABOUT PRAYER I learned from the poor of the Caribbean.

Hearing a mother pray for "daily bread" to feed her hungry children, I learned the importance of having faith in the face of desperate uncertainty.

Watching a horribly scarred leper offer prayers of thanksgiving for our beautiful world, I learned the joy of surrendering to God.

Listening to an old woman praise the Lord for a miracle performed, I learned to respect the promises and power of God.

Seeing serenity in the face of a missionary who had committed his life to serving the needy, I learned how prayer can be a wellspring of God's mercy and peace.

As the director of the Christian relief agency Food For The Poor, I often travel to the Caribbean to visit with the poor and the missionaries who serve in impoverished communities. I treasure these trips because I value the spiritual perspective of the men and women I meet in the slums. Most of them are simple people, unfettered by the influences of materialism, and their theology is direct and uncomplicated. There is God. There is the family. There is prayer.

Visiting the Caribbean's poor and seeing life from their perspective can be very challenging for a First-World Christian. The experience compels you to reevaluate your life and priorities. Am I taking God seriously? Have I surrendered myself to him, or do I struggle against his will? Do I look forward to prayer as an intimate time of sharing with my Father, or has it become just an empty routine? Am I on the right path in my spiritual journey, or has the road I've chosen taken me away from God and his purpose for my life?

By allowing me to see the world through their eyes, the poor have taught me to see God and my life in a whole new light. Their living lessons in faith, love, and surrender have blessed me and strengthened my personal relationship with the Lord.

Frequently I'm able to share this experience by taking small groups of Food For The Poor supporters on trips to the Caribbean—not on luxury vacations but on "pilgrimages" to meet the poor in Haiti and Jamaica. I'm excited about this book because it will allow many more people to share in the powerful experience of a Caribbean pilgrimage.

Through the stories in this book, we meet the poor and also the heroic men and women who serve them. We share the faith of men, women, and children who depend on prayer and God's mercy for their daily survival. We hear the testimony of pastors, priests, nuns, and other people who live and work among the poor. We see prayer as a channel of both divine guidance and miracles of deliverance.

Ultimately, the pilgrimage takes us back to the fundamentals of our faith. It teaches us, in simple terms, everything we need to know about prayer, its promise and power.

Ferdinand Mahfood

PREFACE

WHAT AM I DOING HERE? I must have asked myself this question a dozen times in the course of my "pilgrimage" to Haiti and Jamaica to gather the interviews for this book.

Much of the time my question was an exclamation of shock. No matter that I had seen many photos of starving children and sick and homeless individuals. Nothing could have prepared me for the sights and sounds and smells of the poverty I was now seeing firsthand, for the oppressiveness and depth of it.

Nor could I brush this off as some overwhelming but impersonal evil. Mercilessly, my conversations with the poor and with the people who serve them confronted me with a poverty that has a name and a face. It might have been possible to put out of my mind the suffering of anonymous crowds in a shantytown. It is not easy to forget Lourdie, who may not have found food for her children today, or to stop wondering whether Althea is still living in a plastic tent.

What am I doing here? Sometimes, though, my question expressed the awe and sense of privilege of an eyewitness at a wondrous event. For it was not only poverty that I encountered in these settings of human misery: Jesus was there too, alive in the people whose stories make up this book—in the loving self-sacrifice of those who have devoted their lives to alleviating suffering, in the loving trust of those who suffer.

"Where two or three are gathered in my name, there am I in their midst" (Matthew 18:20). While in Jamaica and Haiti, I discovered that this promise of Jesus applies not only to prayer but also to interviews about prayer. Sometimes as short as fifteen minutes, never longer than two hours, these interviews took place in quite a variety of settings and circumstances: leprosariums, offices, shantytowns, private homes from varied income brackets, soup kitchens, churches, shelters for the homeless. Whatever the setting, Jesus was there. Because of that, conversations which might otherwise have been quite ordinary became moving moments of communion in him. I hope my presentation of these interviews conveys something of this sense of God's presence.

I owe a debt of thanks to Danielle Jean-Felix, without whom I would not have understood the Creole-speaking contributors to this book, and to the staff workers from Food For The Poor's offices in Port-au-Prince, Haiti, and Kingston, Jamaica, who organized my visits and shepherded me from one interview to the next. I am also grateful for the professional expertise of Gina Fontana, Food For The Poor's staff photographer. Gina's sensitive photographs of the people in this book are an indispensable accompaniment to their prayers, stories, and profiles.

Finally, to all these contributors, I am more grateful than I can say. Their openness and willingness to reveal something of how they relate to God is what made this book possible. Each interview left me enriched in some way. I hope that readers will have the same experience and that, through their encounter with these brothers and sisters, they too will learn about prayer.

Louise Perrotta

CHAPTER ONE

Lord, Make Me More Like You

Anyone who prays this prayer has glimpsed something powerfully attractive about God. This is true of the people introduced in this chapter. Having caught a glimpse of God, they have fallen in love with him and have set out after him.

But no one whose eyes have been opened in this way wants to stop with merely seeing, or even following God. And indeed, for all of us—no matter how clear or how dim our vision of God—something planted deep within us cries out for fulfillment: we want to be united with the One in whose image we were created. "Our hearts are restless, O Lord," wrote St. Augustine, "and they will not rest until they rest in you." Amazingly, this union that we long for is precisely what God has in mind. *"As you, Father, are in me and I am in you, may they also be in us..."* is what Jesus prayed for us just before he gave up his life on the cross (John 17:21).

There is a choice before us here—one that we express daily through a host of minor choices related to friends, activities, thoughts, attitudes, prayer. These everyday decisions put us on one of two paths. On one, God's image in us will be dimmed, blurred, eventually obscured. On the other, we are revealed as shining images of God, transformed by him "from one degree of glory to another" (2 Corinthians 3:18).

The people whose stories appear here have made their choice, each in their own way, to be drawn by love farther and farther down that sometimes painful, always joyful, road that leads to union with God.

Prayer for a Father's Heart

YOU WATCH HIM WALKING through the courtyard of his vocational school, surrounded by lively boys in red-and-white-checked shirts. They all want his attention, and each one gets it. A pat on the back, an arm around the shoulders, a playful punch, a "Joseph, how's the stomach?" You are seeing fatherly love in action.

This is Attilio Stra, Salesian missionary to Haiti for the past twenty years. He has traveled a long way from his native Turin, Italy, to be a father to these homeless boys he has rescued from the streets of Port-au-Prince. But perhaps his interior journey has been the longer one.

"I am always asking God to give me and maintain in me what he promises in the Bible," says Father Stra, "a heart of flesh to replace my heart of stone. Because only such a heart can truly love—and without this love, it would be worse than a waste of time to try and help the boys. Better I should take up some kind of manual labor—build chairs or something—than try and build men without relying on God's love."

You wouldn't guess it, but almost all of the smiling boys who step forward so eagerly to welcome you with a handshake have had their lives turned upside down by some tragedy. One ran away from his mountain village after his father was murdered in a land dispute. Another was hit by a car and is finally recovering after barely pulling through two operations. Still another was hardened by five years on the streets—especially by a two-year stint as water boy to the local prostitutes and their clients. Still another was traumatized by the shock of seeing his father kill his mother with a machete.

"Only God's love, over time, can heal wounds so deep,"

Playful young hands rest affectionately on a balding head at Father Attilio Stra's home for street boys in Haiti. "It's not enough to talk to the boys or work with them," Father Stra often reminds his staff. "We must pray for them. And the greater the problems they give us, the more we must place them in the heart of the Good Shepherd, with trust that he will not lose a single one."

says Father Stra. That they do heal is a constant cause of wonderment for the priest, and it motivates him to continue.

Father Stra is deeply convinced of the primary importance of the family. "Even a mediocre family can provide things that our home cannot," he maintains. He goes to great lengths to reconcile each of the boys with their parents, in some cases traveling for days by boat and jeep and on foot to reach them. For this reason he is especially moved when family relationships are set right.

"Such healings may not be very visible or spectacular, but they are the real miracles," says Father Stra. A mother who thought her son was dead sees him return after three years to ask her forgiveness for running away. A son who used to say, "I hate my father, and I'm going to kill him," learns to forgive his parent and pray for him daily. A boy who once refused any contact with his family now works hard to earn a little money so that he can take a gift home at Easter break—a pack and a half of cigarettes for his father, a pair of underpants for his grandmother.

"Simple things—almost ridiculous sometimes," says Father Stra, "but signs that hearts are being transformed supernaturally. Many times we think that religion is just going to church or reciting prayers. But a child whose actions express love, sharing, and forgiveness is being religious. He is on the right path of Jesus."

Father Stra looks for these signs of conversion in his own heart, too. "How can I possibly educate the boys to give up violence, hatred, and sloth, unless I myself am doing the same? This is a lesson I must teach with my whole life, not just my words.

"And how can I possibly love the boys unless I am allowing the Lord to change my heart?"

Father Stra speaks of his boys with such pride and warmth

and deep concern. Does he ever have trouble loving them?

Oh yes, he assures you. Selfless, humble, constant love is a challenge. "It's not always easy to love. Sure, it's no problem when people are as you wish them to be. But to truly love—to respect them as they are, to accept them when they give you problems—this is impossible without God's gift of a new heart."

And so, addressing God as *Bondye*, the Creole title he learned from his boys, Attilio Stra asks his Father for a father's heart.

Bondye Papa! **Dear Lord! Dad!**
You once promised to change hearts of stone into hearts of flesh.
Here is my heart once again.
Change and keep this heart so that it will keep loving you and loving those you have given me to love.

**Keep in me a heart that welcomes and understands,
that respects each child as he is—not as I wish him to be or as a projection of myself;
a heart that always dares to hope and have faith;
a vulnerable, sensitive heart that can still be surprised, and even afraid sometimes.**

**Dear Lord, you know how much it frightens me when I meet people
—mothers and fathers, priests and nuns—
whose hearts have grown cold and bitter with the years.**
They have forgotten how to be open, how to share and learn.
**They have lost their sense of astonishment and wonder:
about each child's suffering,
about their every small step towards you,
about your love.**

I am weak, dear Lord, and I know this could happen to me.
Things can get routine.
I can start thinking in terms of "cases" and "problem
   children."
I can feel resentful sometimes when I am opposed or
   ignored
   or made to feel that I am getting old and useless.
Preserve me from such hardheartedness,
   for I would rather live no longer on this earth
   than to live here with a stony heart.

So I ask you again: keep in me a heart that loves,
   a humble heart that accepts, a heart that smiles.
And may that smile ever remain in my eyes,
   which are the mirrors of the heart.

To this, my prayer, dear Father, please say Amen: "I agree!"

"Prayer is like breathing: you cannot live without it," says Sister of Mercy Regina Burrichter. "It's like a mother who has a son thousands of miles away on the battlefront. She may be doing many things—ironing, putting up curtains, cooking a meal—but her mind is never off her son. May I always do likewise."

Fanning Flickering Flames

MOST OF US WANT NO SHARE of other people's suffering. *My own is enough, thank you.* But ten years ago Sister Regina Burrichter felt the stirrings of a surprising desire. She was doing social justice work in a Massachusetts parish at the time, helping various groups to organize against discrimination. "It was important work, but I felt removed from the suffering of individual people," she says. "It didn't touch me personally."

That's a problem? It was for Sister Regina, who found within herself a growing yearning for more direct contact with the dire poverty and need that afflict so many of the world's peoples. "I wanted to share more closely in such suffering, so that I might become more compassionate, more sensitized to the suffering Christ, and more like him—and always, I wanted to bring new hope." In 1988 that desire led Sister Regina to Jamaica.

Today you can find her at Atonement Catholic Church, in Waterford, just west of Kingston. That is, you can find her there on Sundays and Mondays, giving Scripture teachings, finding ways to link the parish's better-off members with the desperately poor who live in the area, making herself available to talk "to anybody about anything." Other days you'll have to track her down somewhere in a wider territory, as she pursues her dizzying schedule. Neighborhood Bible studies, all-day visitation of the sick, food distribution, classes and workshops of various types, home visits to assess housing and other needs—it's all in a week's work for Sister Regina.

Organized she may be, but there is nothing routine about how this energetic nun responds to the suffering she sees on her rounds. "I'll never *be* one of these poor people. I'll probably never live at that level of misery. But to *feel* with them," Sister Regina says with warmth—"I guess that's what I keep praying for." Cases like the following provide her with ample training.

I've known Sylvia for several years now. She's a frail woman, a single mother with three children by two different fathers. Her daughter is normal, but her sons are severely retarded. They look like emaciated children of twelve or thirteen, though they're twenty-three and twenty-six; they can't make human sounds, but grunt like animals. They are totally incapable of caring for themselves. Sylvia has no one to help her, and can't afford to pay anyone to look in on her sons while she goes off to her low-income job. So they stay home alone all day, tied to the bed, locked up in the house from seven in the morning till six at night with not a bite to eat or a drop to drink.

Sylvia really loves these boys, and when I went to visit her two weeks ago, I found her deeply discouraged about their situation. She had hit rock bottom and her pain was beyond all tears. It struck me that she was truly like a broken reed. My meditation later that day was on Psalm 34, and I begged the Lord to awaken and sharpen my senses so that I could "taste and see" a little bit of Sylvia's suffering. "I want to feel what she's feeling, Lord. Let me feel her pain and, through it, your own. And let that pain spur me to action. I don't want this to be just an intellectualized prayer, but something that's in my blood—prayer with guts in it."

Sylvia's pain went into me sufficiently to become a part of my prayer, and that prayer spilled over into action. Soon after I found a woman who was willing to look in on Sylvia's sons during the day. She's taking a lot of initiative and is now working with Sylvia to get medical attention for them.

Sylvia's story is instructive in that it reveals so much about how Sister Regina prays. Suffering and identifying with Jesus in the poor has become such a big focus that what the nun offers God in her own personal prayer is what the poor offer him—namely, their specific sufferings, along with their sense of God's mysterious presence in their lives.

None of this is abstract for Sister Regina. Every suffering has a name and a face and, if you ask, she will express this for you in her adaptation of a song that is used in her parish. (She loves to sing!) The refrain asks, "What do I have to offer my Lord?" and the original verses answer: "I have my love… my heart…my song…my life…my soul…my dream." In Sister Regina's version, the answers are different and they are spoken by the people she describes here:

"I have my pain"—Regina Cristobal: This is a young woman who has needed medical attention for a long time but can't afford it. She has a kidney problem, I think, and is in ongoing pain, but every bit of money she can come by goes to her children. She's a very religious person. Her shack is decorated with every kind of prayer imaginable! Lives on a dirt lane with no name. Well, I never noticed a name until the last time I visited, when I saw a signpost that said, Godly Avenue. Regina's doing, of course. "I just got to thinking that this is what this street is going to be," she told me, "so I got a young man to put up the sign." And Godly Avenue it will likely remain—especially if Regina keeps living on it!

"I have one meal a day"—Clive Thompson: Clive is a farmer who's been pulling himself up by his bootstraps. One afternoon I went out to the field where he had been working since five in the morning. "What have you had to eat today?" I asked him. Nothing besides a cup of tea, I discovered. And dinner would be rice, with perhaps something to flavor it. Twice a week only, Clive and his wife permit themselves to eat some of the vegetables they grow: "Not many. We need to sell all we can."

"I have eviction"—Marlene Allen: Marlene has a decent house now, but what she used to offer the Lord as her daily prayer were the eviction threats she kept receiving from her landlady. Not that Marlene's shack was any castle. In fact, it was the second worst living situation I've seen in all these years of going in and out of poor houses. Rotten wood, rusted zinc, rats everywhere, an overflowing pit toilet, a cramped room maybe three feet by five—these are the conditions in which Marlene was struggling to raise four children, one of them severely retarded.

"I have a plastic tent"—Althea Hook: This twenty-nine-year-old mother and her four children were burned out of their last house and now live in a makeshift shelter with no more protection from the elements than four plastic sides and a plastic roof. "How do you talk to the Lord about this problem, Althea?" I asked her. Very simply, she replied, "I tell him, 'Lord, help me get a job. Help me to earn something for me and my children. There's nowhere to live. This plastic tent is terrible when rain comes; it wets up.'" Althea cried here, and I cried with her later in my own prayers because she went on to say: "Sometimes I give up. I tell the Lord, 'When my children cry and nothing to eat... Lord, before you suffer them more, take them back.'"

"I have nowhere for myself"—Beverly Cole: Beverly has never known what it means to be part of a family; she's been in institutions for the homeless all twenty-three years of her life. Her situation right now is terrible. She's pregnant and living in the overcrowded family home of the young man who fathered her child. He's disowned Beverly, though, and she's afraid that she'll be put out on the street. Somehow, she can still pray with thanks and hope: "Jesus, thank you for bringing me through the past. Thank you for what you've given me. When my baby comes in December, I know God will do some more for me if I help myself."

"I have sickness in my house"—Inez Francis: A most beautiful woman in her late sixties, Inez lives way up in the hills. Her husband is in exceedingly poor health, her forty-one-year-old son is mentally retarded, and she's the only able-bodied worker in the family. Almost every week she travels up and down those hills to see me and get ideas about what to do. I helped her apply for a chicken raising project and she's doing very well: has already raised and sold two sets of one hundred chickens and is waiting for her third set. Inez is extremely religious and her faith inspires me.

Direct, day-in, day-out contact with such profound pain helps her touch the Paschal mystery, says Sister Regina. "That means suffering *and* resurrection!" she stresses. "There's the hope of the next life and also hope for enduring through present sufferings with the life that comes from Christ."

Through Inez and Althea and Clive and the other people she encounters, Sister Regina says she has grown. "They make my prayer life better; they make me a better religious, a better human being."

Sister Regina aims to reciprocate in kind. "From teen years, my favorite saying has been, 'It is better to light one candle than to curse the darkness.' Now I add my own saying: 'Be the Paschal candle for others.' I want to plant and cultivate hope."

I live with three other Sisters of Mercy. Last weekend one of them—who, for seven years, has heard the stories I share at table about the people I meet—said to me, "I now have your pet name." (Everybody in Jamaica gets a pet name sooner or later.) "It's *FFF*." Now, when I was a child, such a nickname could only have meant something like Flat-Footed Florence! I held my breath and wondered if I had been walking funny. But when she explained the name, it was such a happy moment for me. "You are Fanning Flickering Flames," she said.

Her pet name is, in fact, a good description of what Sister Regina hopes to do with the people she meets. "Many are so hopeless, frustrated, ready to give up. The flame is almost out." But with the grace of God, a deep prayer life, and the help of various organizations, Sister Regina keeps after her goal: "to give the new hope that comes from a life of living close to Christ; to give another light; to fan flames that are flickering and ready to go out."

"It's simple, it's effective, and it keeps me growing in the Lord."

My ABCD of Prayer

IF YOU COUNT HIS FIVE-YEAR APPRENTICESHIP, Reverend Luther Gibbs has served as a Baptist minister for fifty years. In that half century he has pastored many churches—preaching, teaching, counseling, building, developing outreach programs, and doing everything else that comprises effective ministry. Reverend Gibbs is "retired" now, but you can still find him on assignment, serving a small new congregation.

He is full of enthusiasm for this latest undertaking, New Haven Baptist Church. For many reasons, this church has been a specific answer to prayer, he says, with a wave of the hand toward a pleasant, spacious building. "We began this out of nothing. You should have seen this place. It was a bog!" Reverend Gibbs has long experience of building churches without money—and of seeing the Lord provide. "You just see the job, do it, and pray for each thing as you need it," he says with a slight smile.

Development is occurring on the spiritual level too, he says. The congregation is small, but a good one-third of its fifty-five members show up for a time of prayer every Wednesday evening.

That is important to Reverend Gibbs, because prayer is so important to him. A careful man with a soft-spoken voice and a deliberate manner, Reverend Gibbs emphasizes his points about prayer with sharp taps of his pen on the table before him.

"My whole life has been centered around prayer," he explains. He credits this to the influence of his mother, "a great Christian lady who taught each of her five children how

A pastor for fifty years, Reverend Luther Gibbs, leader of New Haven Baptist Church in Kingston, Jamaica, prays to God in his own words but also likes to read the prayers of other men and women of faith. One of his favorites is the well-known Serenity Prayer by Reinhold Niebuhr (1892-1971), a theologian and voice for social justice:

O God, give us the serenity to accept what cannot be changed,
courage to change what should be changed,
and wisdom to distinguish one from the other.

to pray. From an early age, I was convinced of the need for prayer."

Reverend Gibbs prays so that he will be changed and empowered by the Source of life. To explain how he views prayer, he likes to tell a story he heard from a preacher years ago.

Once there were two streams standing at the foot of a mountain. On top of the mountain was a great lake and in front of it, a great desert.

Both streams wanted to water the desert, and one day they began to deliberate about how to go about it. "I think that to be successful, we must find a way to climb the mountain and get attached to the lake," said one stream. "Man, what a waste of time!" the other stream retorted. "You'll never make it. And besides, look at all this parched land just crying out for water. I'm going on."

So the second stream flowed out into the desert. As the sun got hotter and hotter and the land dryer and dryer, the stream got smaller and smaller. Eventually it faded because it had no resources.

In the meantime, the first stream was struggling up the mountain. It was a long, arduous climb, but finally the stream joined the lake and asked, "Will you help me to go out and water the desert?" "I will," was the answer. So together lake and stream flowed down the mountain and into the desert, making the dry land rich and fertile.

"Prayer helps me to do what that stream did," explains Reverend Gibbs, "to make myself one with the resource of the lake. Because of it, my life and ministry have been watered constantly by the Spirit of God, and I haven't dried up after fifty years!"

Discipline and diligence characterize Reverend Gibbs' approach to personal prayer.

Ever since I was in my early twenties, I've set aside a quiet time for personal prayer every morning. I heard a preacher say once that you should never let the birds get to the dew before you get to the Lord in prayer, and so I talk to the Lord first thing, before I do anything else. That's usually around five o'clock, right after I wake up. I kneel and pray by my bed, then I make myself a cup of tea and go into my study to do some reading and meditation.

There isn't a day that I don't read the Bible! I've studied it and gone through it over and over again, and I can always find something to give me strength and courage. I use a study guide to keep me focused—something that comments on a particular passage and also has suggestions for prayer. I use other books too: practical helps for Christian living, inspirational biographies and stories, and collections of prayers of great men and women.

Though I like to read other peoples' prayers, I speak to the Lord in my own words, using a pattern that I learned long ago. You might call it my ABCD of prayer.

I begin with *A*, which stands for *Adoration*. I recognize that I am in the presence of God, who is holy, majestic, and powerful—able to meet every need.

B is for *Blessing*, which means recognizing what God has done for me and blessing and praising him for it. I bless him for the renewal and refreshment of a good night's sleep, for the new day and the opportunities it brings, for the good things of the day before, and for whatever else is on my mind.

Then I turn to *C*, *Confession* I admit my sins and ask forgiveness for them. Here it helps me to think of certain biblical figures: David, a great warrior and a man after God's own heart, who prayed, "Against you only have I sinned"; Paul, a tireless apostle who nonetheless prayed, "When I would do good, evil is

present.... O wretched man that I am! Who shall deliver me?";
and Peter, who exclaimed, "Depart from me, Lord, for I am a
sinful man!" These men all realized something of their inner sin-
fulness before God, who sees into every heart. And so though
people might say, "Oh, Reverend Gibbs is such a nice man,"
God sees deeper. I am wayward and sinful—so my confession is
long!

And there is also a *D* to my prayer: *Desire* in which I express
my petitions to God. First I pray for others—for my family and
congregation and all the people I know, for the country, for various causes. Then I pray for myself—for all the day's events, for
strength and insight, for specific needs.

Here, in my petition for personal change, I also pray for four
more C's. I ask God to make me *Careful* so that whatever I do I
will do well and exercise care towards people in my behavior and
attitude. I pray to be *Confident* and ready to move ahead wherever God leads. I ask the Lord to make me *Calm* in difficult situations and able to seek solutions wisely. Finally, I pray that I will
always be *Committed* to God. And here I can say that although I
have often felt droopy and weak, there has never been a day in
my Christian life when I have felt opposed to God. I have made
mistakes, but I have always desired to be with the Lord.

Daily personal prayer is what has helped me to stay at the
Lord's side. It is the secret to whatever success I have experienced in these fifty years of ministry.

"Prayer is simply the intimate relationship that I have with the Lord," says Brother Thomas Dynetius, who belongs to the Missionaries of the Poor, a developing religious community that serves society's outcasts. "Moments spent with him in personal prayer are always precious, always too short." Here Brother Thomas has put aside his informal, workaday habit for the monastic robe that the Missionaries wear for liturgical functions.

Sometimes, in a glance, you discover him.

A Glimpse of Jesus in Disguise

ALL THE MISERIES OF HUMANITY seem to have gathered in the courtyard of Faith Centre. Elderly people slump in wheelchairs. A man with one leg shakes his cane at a deaf and dumb boy. A wild-eyed woman you have never seen before accosts you with a demand for "what you said you were going to bring me." She retreats as a tough-looking young man with a bandaged head wound pushes past.

Yet there is a certain peace here. At its center are a few young men moving about, responding patiently to cries for help, facing the press of needs with compassion and patience. Each wears a white or beige or blue shirt, khaki pants, sandals, and around his neck a wooden cross with the face of Christ carved on it.

They are Missionaries of the Poor, a fledgling community that is on its way to becoming a religious order in the Catholic Church. The group was started in 1981 when Father Richard Holung, a Jamaican and Jesuit, invited two other priests to join him in serving society's outcasts. Fifty-four men now belong to the community, which has houses in Haiti, India, the Philippines, and Jamaica, where it maintains four homes for the homeless, including Faith Centre.

Brother Thomas Dynetius, twenty-seven, encountered the Missionaries of the Poor in his native India. He joined them about three years ago out of a desire "to serve the poor more deeply and commit myself more closely to the Lord." Since then his days have been filled with service and, of course, prayer.

Brother Thomas verifies the impression you immediately formed of the difficulty of caring for the residents of Faith

Centre: "It is really demanding work." And perhaps even more demanding than the actual work is the Missionaries' intention to serve with compassion, for Christ's sake.

"We cannot merely *tolerate* these people as we take care of them," Brother Thomas explains. "It is our mission to see Christ in each one of them and therefore to love them. Only then will we be able to treat them with the respect they deserve. We are not social workers. Social workers take care of people without necessarily feeling called to love them. With us, it's different."

No wonder Brother Thomas goes on to speak of prayer as "the backbone of our life, the sustenance of our soul, the guide that keeps us on the right track"!

Only with the personal transformation that comes through prayer could you come to see Christ in "Lazarus," for example. That's the name the Missionaries gave to one of the men who now makes his home at Faith Centre. They literally picked him up off a downtown street in September 1992. Beaten up in a fight, he had been lying there for a week with thousands of people stepping around him every day as they went about their business. Finally alerted to the problem, the Missionaries took Lazarus in, bathed him, and patiently picked all the maggots out of his wounds: "His head was covered with them; they were eating him up." Truly, love called this man back from the dead!

So every day Brother Thomas and his associates pray "that the Lord would help me love." Always faith tells them that they are serving the suffering Christ as they tend to his suffering people. Occasionally some personal experience reinforces this truth. Sometimes you really do see the Lord in the poor, Brother Thomas has discovered. And sometimes, too, the poor may catch a glimpse of Christ in these Missionaries who serve them....

One day when I was at Jacob's Well, one of our centers here in Kingston, a man in his thirties walked in asking for some food. He had another need that he wasn't aware of: he was completely covered with some kind of soot or dirt and oil and desperately needed a bath. I couldn't help thinking, *This man is so dirty that I don't want to touch him or have him touch me!* So I looked at him and walked away. But just then one of the brothers called out to me, "Brother Thomas! Show this man where he can take a bath. He doesn't need help. Just show him the place and give him what he needs."

So I led the grimy man to the bathroom and told him to get started while I went back for soap. "I'm finished," he announced when I returned a few minutes later. "You are?" I said with surprise. The sooty coating was undisturbed, and his skin color hadn't changed a bit.

I felt an inner prodding. *Thomas, he needs a good bath.* I made a quick decision. "Let me do this for you, man," I said. And I grabbed the soap and began lathering and scrubbing him.

At some point in the process I looked up and caught the expression on the man's face. How can I describe his look? There was something deeper than surprise in it. Was it wonder that someone would care enough about him to render such a service? Did he see Jesus in me and experience Jesus' love for him through me? Whatever it was, this man had the look of someone who was being touched by God.

What I do know with more certainty is what happened to me at that moment. In a flash of recognition I saw Christ in the face of the man I was bathing.

Later that evening when I went to pray, that face kept coming back to me. I just couldn't put it out of my mind. Seeing Christ in the poor—an ideal I had often reflected on—had suddenly taken on vivid meaning. Serving the poor had become more satisfying, so comforted was I to think that God would indeed work through me to reveal his love to others.

Every once in a while I still catch sight of this poor man, this Jesus in disguise. He's on the street again and filthier than ever. But I no longer look on his thick layers of grime with disgust. Instead they evoke memories of a fateful bath and a face I will never forget—and I am heartened to keep serving the Lord at all times, even when he remains hidden.

Brother Thomas Dynetius likes to use Scripture as the basis for his prayer. One of his favorite passages comes from the Old Testament book of Hosea. The prophet is describing ancient Israel's rejection of God in favor of false gods but "this describes *my* life!" says Brother Thomas. "So often *I* go away from the Lord, but he is always there to take me back in his love."

As Brother Thomas reflects on this passage, it becomes a prayer of petition for personal change, especially in his work with the poor: "God calls me to return to him with a broken heart—not a heart which loses hope but one which longs to be filled with his love so that this same love may be poured out; not just to get a job done but to be another Christ for the people, imitating his example of compassionate love."

> When Israel was a child, I loved him,
> and out of Egypt I called my son.
> The more I called them,
> the more they went from me....
> Yet it was I who taught Ephraim to walk,
> I took them up in my arms;
> but they did not know that I healed them.
> I led them with cords of human kindness,
> with bands of love.

I was to them like those
    who lift infants to their cheeks.
I bent down to them and fed them....

My heart recoils within me;
    my compassion grows warm and tender.
I will not execute my fierce anger;
    I will not again destroy Ephraim;
for I am God and no mortal,
    the Holy One in your midst,
    and I will not come in wrath.

HOSEA 11:1-2, 3-4, 8-9

CHAPTER TWO

You Guide Me Along the Right Path

Look over the "how to" section in any large bookstore and you will find ample evidence that people are hungry for guidance on every topic imaginable. Where should I invest my money? How can I lose twenty pounds? What is an effective way to reach noncommunicative children? Who gives the best advice about making a career change?

Of course, it is not only the "expert" authors of such books who get consulted about matters like this. In practice, most people look closer to home for their guidance and seek it first from people they know—relatives, friends, members of the clergy, business associates, and other advisors.

While not neglecting the counsel of other people, the men and women in this chapter demonstrate an approach to guidance that wise old Ben Sira describes in the Old Testament book of Sirach (Ecclesiasticus in many Bibles): "But above all, pray to the Most High that he may direct your way in truth" (37:15). These people pray about everything: major life decisions, routine challenges, basic needs, crises.

Their stories reveal a few of the many ways through which God directs us. Sometimes guidance comes through an inner voice or urge that is recognized as the prompting of the Holy Spirit. Sometimes it comes naturally—almost imperceptibly—

as a situation evolves. Sometimes it is revealed in a sense of peace or rightness about a particular course of action. Sometimes it is indicated through circumstances that just "happen" to fall together.

How best to receive God's guidance? These stories show the way: stay close to Jesus in prayer and lay every perplexing situation at his feet.

Guidance can be a life-and-death matter.

Her Eyes Are on the Lord

WHAT IS IT ABOUT talking to Anna Baptiste that sets echoes of the psalms running through your head? Perhaps it is her readiness to express need. Like the psalmists—and unlike many who are just as needy but slower to reveal it—Anna cries out to God, making her petition without holding back.

Anna's prayer also recalls the psalms by its admission of absolute dependence on God. "How hard it is for the rich to depend on the Lord," a rabbi once said. "All their possessions cry out, 'Depend on us!'" But Anna has nothing with which to mask her need, and so this temptation does not characterize her relationship with God.

One of the naked needs for which Anna depends on God is guidance. Nothing high-flown or abstract here—just plain and simple direction about how to keep herself and her loved ones alive. For this reason, Anna's prayer, like the psalms, strikes a basic and universal note.

I have six children—two boys and four girls. My husband hasn't been able to find work in five years. Me either. I used to make a little money as a street vendor, but the things I was selling got too expensive for me to buy. I have many problems.

> How long, O Lord, will you look on?
> Rescue me…!
> You have seen, O Lord; do not be silent!
> O Lord, do not be far from me! PSALMS 35:17, 22

We have no house of our own, and that means we have to move around a lot. Right now we're using the house of a

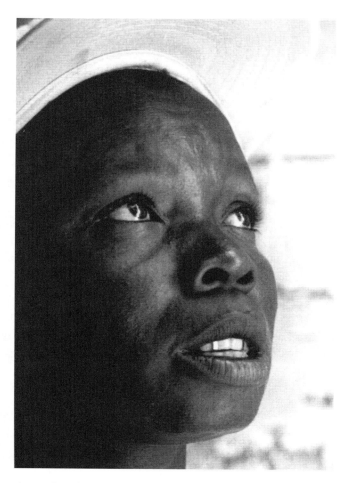

Anna Baptiste, mother of six, lives in a run-down section of Port-au-Prince, Haiti. Her simple cries to God evoke the prayers of the psalmists who lived in ancient Israel.

relative who's in the Dominican Republic. When she comes back, she'll take the house away, and we'll move on somewhere else. I've asked God to find me a stable place for my family, but so far we're still living with other people.

> **Lord, my wanderings you have noted;**
> **you have kept a record of my tears.** PSALMS 56:8

Sometimes I feel I would like to put shoes on my kids' feet, and then I would like to send them to school. But if they could go today, they probably couldn't go tomorrow, because I can't keep them dressed appropriately for school. They keep outgrowing their shoes and their clothes, and I can't afford to buy more.

> **You have seen this trouble and sorrow,**
> **you note it, you take it in hand.** PSALMS 10:14

I say to God, "I don't know why I am suffering. Why do I have so many problems? Is it my sin that closed the door on me?"

> **Do not forsake me, O Lord;**
> **O my God, do not be far from me;**
> **make haste to help me,**
> **O Lord, my salvation.** PSALMS 38:21-22

Every day I call out to God in the morning, at noon, and at night. I spread out a piece of canvas on the floor and I get down on my knees or lie down on it. Each time I pray, tears flow from my eyes.

> **But I call upon God,**
> **and the Lord will save me.**

> Evening, morning, and at noon,
> I utter my complaint and moan,
> and he will hear my voice.   PSALMS 55:17-18

I say to God, "I am in your hands. Do what you will with me. And my children—I am not their owner. You have given them to me to hold for you.

"Lord, what am I going to give your children to eat today?"

> But as for me I trust in you, O Lord.
> I say, "You are my God."
> My life is in your hands.   PSALMS 31:14-15

When I have a need for my kids, I ask God what to do, and he shows me all sorts of ways to find what I need. God gives me ideas.

> I will instruct you and teach you
> the way you should go.
> I will counsel you with my eye upon you.
>   PSALMS 32:8

One day after praying like this, I was walking down the street and I saw a lady holding some little cards. I got the feeling that I should talk to her, and when I did, I found out that she was registering people to receive free food. I applied, and I qualified, so ever since then I've been able to get food for my kids five days a week.

> The Lord gives food to all living things,
> for his steadfast love endures forever.
>   PSALMS 136:25

I always ask God to guide me, but sometimes he gives me a test to see if I will follow him instead of something else. He wants to see where I am in my faith, so he puts me in front of a choice. Will I go left or right? Will I take the good path? Like sometimes when your child is sick, God wants to see if you will trust him or if you will take that child to a voodoo priest instead.

> **I have kept the way of the Lord**
> **and have not been disloyal to my God.**
>
> PSALMS 18:21

So I talk to God about all my problems. "I have no money. I can't buy food. My children are sick." And I tell him, "It's not me who knows what to do. You have to show me." And when he answers my prayer, I kneel down and I thank him for all he does. I always finish my prayer by singing this: "O Rock of Ages, you will never change. When I am still, sometimes my heart is sad, and tears stream from my eyes. And when I feel alone with many problems, tears stream from my eyes."

> **Like the eyes of a servant**
> **on the hand of her mistress,**
> **so our eyes are on the Lord our God,**
> **till he show us his mercy.**   PSALMS 123:2

When I pray, I feel stronger. I have more love and courage. And even when I am hungry or thirsty, if I pray and sing I feel strong and have more faith in God. And I can say to him, "Lord, whatever your will is, I accept it."

> **Truly the eye of the Lord is on those**
> **who fear him,**

on those who hope in his steadfast love,
to deliver their soul from death,
and to keep them alive in famine.

Our soul waits for the Lord;
he is our help and shield.
Our heart is glad in him,
because we trust in his holy name.
Let your steadfast love, O Lord,
be upon us,
even as we hope in you.   PSALMS 33:18-22

*"The charred boards stood as a reminder
of the night God visited our house."*

The Spirit's Urgent Prompting

JOHN LEVY LEANS FORWARD IN HIS CHAIR and declares himself "quite fascinated" by the invitation to discuss "this very important subject of prayer." He is sitting in his office in the St. Andrew Settlement, an outreach project of the Anglican parish church of St. Andrew, in Kingston, Jamaica. John's obvious enthusiasm for the topic makes you suspect that if these walls could speak, they would tell of many prayers offered here.

John has directed the Settlement since its founding in 1965. Medical and dental clinics, self-help projects, feeding programs, educational and recreational facilities—in these and other ways, John and his staff and volunteers bring the hope and love of Jesus Christ into this economically depressed and densely populated area.

Whatever good the Settlement has been able to do John attributes to God's guidance received through prayer. "My belief in prayer is absolute," he says. "We have a saying in Jamaica that water is life. I would like to add that prayer is life. I fail to see how one could exist without it."

John's schedule reflects this belief. He and his wife, Vincenti, get up at four o'clock every morning to begin the day by talking to God together. "We talk to the Lord about specific things, asking for his blessing and direction." Because of prayer, John says, "I have seen very clearly the direction that God has given—both for my work and my personal life."

As a young man I had two major decisions to make. First, I wanted to get married, and so I was very concerned to find a

John and Vincenti Levy begin every day by praying together. "Neglecting prayer gives me a sense of unease," says John. "For me, prayer is life!"

suitable wife. But where would I meet her, and when? I prayed earnestly to God about this for a long time: "Please find the right person!" I didn't describe her, but I had visions of someone just like Vincenti. When we finally met, at a youth camp, I knew.... Now, after thirty-six years of marriage, the fact that God guided me to this woman who has been such a wonderful wife and mother remains for me the best possible evidence of God's readiness to provide direction.

My second major decision concerned where I should work. God answered that prayer by leading me to the job I now do and have been doing at St. Andrew's Settlement for the last thirty years. Not only that: he has provided guidance for every situation I have encountered here, no matter how difficult.

And it has been extremely difficult at times. One reason is that we work in a community where there are political divisions and tensions that can easily flare up into violence. I have never felt that I should remain sitting at my desk, removed from the situation, whenever such a crisis arose. I have always gone into the area to try and pacify, to help resolve the conflict. But sometimes the atmosphere has been so volatile, so charged with violence, that I feared for my life—especially in my first years here when, as a newcomer, I was regarded with suspicion.

One day about four months after I started this job, an elderly man who was waiting to see the doctor at our health clinic had a heart attack and died. I set out into the neighborhood to try and get in touch with his relatives. As I went from street to street, I noticed groups of people intently reading the evening paper. Since each group I passed was increasingly abusive and menacing, I finally deduced that there must be something in the paper that had to do with me.

There was. It was an expose by a journalist who had come into the community incognito and gathered information about how the people lived. His article highlighted the vice in the neighborhood; it revealed things about the people living here that were highly domestic and personal—so personal that it seemed someone had given him inside information. And since he held up St. Andrew's Settlement as the community's only hope, it looked as though that informer was me!

"Look here, you have told our business for everyone to see," the people accused me. "John Levy, you are a wicked man."

What to do? I put the whole situation into the Lord's hands and asked him to guide me. The upshot was that God brought good out of evil. I was able to convince the people that I had had nothing to do with the exposé and that, in fact, I totally agreed with their point of view. The paper printed a front-page photo of me and some of the community leaders and clearly stated that I had not been the reporter's source of information. Not only did this vindicate me in the people's eyes; it also gained me their confidence as someone who cared about them and took their part.

Many incidents like this have convinced me that if you put your faith in God and yield to him, he shows the way. But the Lord has also given me guidance at times when I wasn't praying for it specifically and didn't even know I needed it.

One evening when our children Elizabeth and Andrew were about five and four, Vincenti and I went out to offer condolences to a friend whose brother had just died. Andrew had a nasal congestion at the time, and the woman who was staying with the children knew what to do if he should have trouble breathing: rub him with a decongestant ointment, plug in the electric tea kettle we had brought into the bedroom, and have him inhale the vapors.

I called the woman frequently during the evening. "Are the children all right?" The answer was always yes. Assured that things were going well, I finally told her that she could go to bed since we would be home soon.

As soon as I hung up the phone, however, I began feeling extremely unsettled. I didn't know what it was, but something wasn't right. "Let's go home," I kept telling Vincenti. "I've just been told that the children are okay, but I'm feeling very uncomfortable."

We heard the children's screams as we drove up to the garage. I raced into their room to find the floor on fire, just inches away from the mosquito netting draped over their bed. That electric kettle had been left on! I got the children out and put out the fire—and then I almost collapsed with fright. To think that if I had ignored those promptings, if we had arrived home only five minutes later, we would have lost Andrew and Elizabeth!

Later we told the story to some visiting friends and one of them, gazing at the burned-out floor, said, "John, never repair this. Let it be a reminder to you of the night God visited your house."

I took his advice. And as long as we lived in that old house, those charred boards always did remind me that the Lord offers protection—and direction—to all who seek him.

Surrounded by children—that's how Sister Mary Benedict Chung has spent most of her nearly fifty years as a Sister of Mercy. Born in Jamaica of Chinese parents, Sister Benedict traces her desire to serve the poor to her mother's example of kindness to those in need.

A split-second prayer saves one child's life—
and turns another's around.

Lord, Do Something!

SISTER MARY BENEDICT CHUNG is talking to a policeman, standing at the gate next to a plaque that reads, "Love serves." It is not yet nine o'clock on this Tuesday morning, and there has already been a shooting in her troubled neighborhood. This was a poor section of Kingston when Sister Benedict began to work here in 1961. It is even poorer now, she says, plagued by unemployment and crime. "Just to survive in this place is a miracle!" But obviously, more than survival has gone on here at the Law Street Training Centre.

Sister Benedict brushes a strand of hair from her face and smooths her apron. She has been wrapping bread in the bakery since 6:30. The bakery, along with a craft and garment-making center, provides jobs and gives people in the neigborhood the skills with which to earn their livelihood. Until recently Sister Benedict handled books, not bread, as principal of the primary school that is also on the compound. Twelve hundred children between the ages of four and twelve attend. Their voices, as they sing and recite their lessons in their classrooms, provide a lively counterpoint to Sister Benedict's remarks.

"None of these buildings was here when I arrived," says Sister Benedict. In fact, she points out, this plot was a wasteland then, a center where robbers from across the gully would store their stolen goods. "Somehow we've been able to develop all this and pay for it. I don't really know how! God has led and provided—and answered our prayers and dreams."

Sister Benedict does not mince words about what has kept her going: "Prayer is my strength. Hanging on and hanging in there, talking to the Lord, knowing he's there for me—that's been my lifeline."

The problems seemed insurmountable at the beginning. Poverty: "You had children fainting from hunger during morning prayers at the school." Hostility, especially from local members of a religious cult: "You had the Rastafarians hurling abuses." Vandalism: "You had people stoning the school and robbing it of stuff." And a bit later, violence: "You had gang warfare, guns firing right and left."

Sister Benedict had her doubts. "I'm never going to last here," she told the Lord. "Maybe I should go home." But as she prayed, she sensed him saying, *Have patience. Take your time. Things will work out. I will lead you.*

"And sure enough," she says, her face breaking into a smile, "the Lord gradually took over. He provided the resources for us to start feeding the children and gave us ideas about how to help their parents improve their lives. He showed us how to make friends with the Rastafarians." (One of them made Sister Benedict a lovely wooden dresser that she cherishes as a sign of this friendship.) "He helped us to gain people's trust. In time, anything that was stolen was always returned. And I especially felt that God was very near when we were able to bring peace between the gangs through dialogue with the leaders. We marked that milestone with a big celebration where both sides came together and shook hands."

How has Sister Benedict experienced the Lord's direction for her life and work? "Most often through ordinary events. Through prayer over a period of time. I talk to the Lord and then I listen. I think that if you give him time, he will always tell you what to do."

But Sister Benedict has also seen God provide guidance in

sudden, dramatic interventions. "It was years ago," she reflects, "but I'll never forget what happened with Aston...."

"Teacher!" The voice came from outside the school classroom where I sat eating lunch with the staff. I looked up to see a little boy peeking in through the window.

"Don't call out to me, Aston," one of the teachers replied. "You've been skipping school again, and you're a naughty boy."

But he persisted, pointing at me. "I see a new sister come. She nice?"

"If you want to find out, come to school."

"All right. I'll come right now."

That's when I got my first good look at Aston. Eight years old, slight build, a wild look in his eye, filthy from head to toe.

"How about getting him washed?" I suggested.

As we cleaned him up and found some clothes to replace his rags, I learned more about Aston. He had no family except an elderly grandmother who couldn't manage him, and he lived on the streets. He earned a little money as a messenger, carrying marijuana from place to place. At night he slept under an old overturned boat on the waterfront.

After we had spruced him up, Aston decided that he would come to school regularly. But in the weeks that followed, I learned what he meant by that: he wanted to spend his days in the principal's office with me! Every morning it was the same thing. Aston would come in, get a little feather duster, crawl under my desk and dust off my shoes.

"Aston, you must go to class!" I would tell him.

"I'm not going to any class. I just want to stay right here with you."

I tried so hard to persuade Aston, prayed so hard about what to do. But he was still a street child, wary and independent.

Then one day when Aston wasn't there, someone burst into my office shouting, "You'd better come fast! There's a street fight going on, and Aston is going to murder someone!"

I ran outside to find Aston gripping a broken bottle with one hand and a terrified child with the other. The jagged edge was only inches from the child's throat.

"Aston, let go!" I cried out, pulling at him. But he struggled like a wild animal and held on all the harder.

Lord, it's your turn, I prayed silently. *Do something!*

But Aston kept his death grip on the boy and fought me off. *Lord, aren't you going to do anything? This is a desperate situation! And I have no idea what to do.*

That's when the thought came to me, in a sudden flash of divine inspiration. *Say something to him.* And I knew what to say.

"Aston, if you love me, give me the bottle."

Aston released the boy and spun around. He grabbed me by the shoulders in a big hug and cried out, "You know I love you. That's why you can ask me for the bottle, and that's why I'm giving it to you." And he handed it over.

God answered my prayers in more ways than one that day, because from then on Aston did attend class. Later, wanting a more stable life, he also decided to let me help him get into a children's home.

I wish I could say that this has a storybook ending, but God's ways are mysterious to us sometimes, and our old habits die hard. Things were going pretty well for Aston until he got into another fight. It was his last. He died of his injuries in the Kingston Public Hospital while I was out of town.

I heard about Aston's last hours from the priest who ministered to him on his deathbed. My little brother died in the Lord, he said.

Many children have come into my life since then, but Aston, who taught me so much about God's guidance and grace, will always hold a special place in my heart. I rejoice to think that I will see him again one day in heaven.

Working in a government agency in Jamaica, Pearline Barrett tries to assess a client's needs. She relies on prayer to guide her in her work with the destitute. "I'm from a family of eleven—a praying family," Pearline declares. This early training in prayer has made all the difference in her personal and professional life, she says.

The Hand of the Almighty

"I REALLY, REALLY, *REALLY* BELIEVE IN PRAYER," says the gracious woman with the warm smile and the gentle eyes. And if you have any doubts at all about Pearline Barrett's affirmation, a quick glance around her office will dismiss them, for Pearl sits surrounded and encompassed by prayers. They are behind her, on wall and bulletin board—a home blessing, a prayer for peace, Scripture verses like, "I can do all things in Christ who strengtheneth me." They are before her, in the desk drawer where Pearl keeps some of her "instruments of peace" close at hand—a worn pocket Bible, an edition of the Psalms, assorted devotional books.

But most of all, you discover, Pearl's prayers are within her, part of her very being. "I'm always communicating with my God," she says. "I walk with him. I talk with him. I give him thanks for everything. As I go through the day, I like to pray certain verses from the Psalms. 'The Lord is my light and my salvation.' I say that a lot. And also, 'In thee, O Lord, do I put my trust.'"

Like any other mother and grandmother (she has four children and six grandchildren), Pearl finds plenty to pray for within her own family. But ever since 1968, when she began working in a government social welfare agency, Pearl's job has been a major incentive to her prayer life. Today, Pearl holds a responsible position in the Poor Relief department, as the agency is called. She oversees a staff of thirteen field workers who serve the needy in two of Jamaica's "parishes," or civil districts, Kingston and St. Andrew.

"We serve the very poor," explains Pearl, "people who are destitute or who are mentally or physically handicapped or who are unable to earn their livelihood." Through home visits, her workers try to help these two thousand adults and one thousand children meet their basic needs for food, clothing, housing, medicine, and schooling. For the even needier people who live on the streets, Pearl and her staff run a shelter and an outreach program that provides breakfast, baths, and medical care.

Briskly, but with a smile for everyone along the way, Pearl gives a quick tour of the women's shelter, empty now at midday. It is spare but neat and clean, every narrow bed covered with a pretty quilt. Each "regular" has decorated her area in her own way, with plants, magazine cutouts, knickknacks, shelves, photos.

"It's become a competition among them! Look at that area now. See how nice it looks? That woman couldn't even make her bed when she first came. She's not quite normal. Hasn't been since the day she came home from market to find her house burned down and her husband and child dead."

Twenty-seven years of dealing with heartbreaking situations like this might make a person either coldly indifferent to human misery or overemotional about it. But Pearl Barrett is neither. In her, motherly compassion and clear-headed efficiency seem to combine in just the right proportions.

How does she manage?

"Well, I enjoy my work. Not that I enjoy seeing people in so much poverty. But I get a lot of satisfaction at being able to help. And most important, I know that I'm not doing this on my own. I'm positive that I'm being led to do what I'm doing—and by no other hand but the hand of the Almighty!"

So every morning when she arrives at work, Pearl takes a moment to put her hand in God's. "Lead me today, Lord," she prays. "Direct me and use me for what you want me to do." Then all the day through she talks to the Lord from the heart, as to a close friend. In moments when she has a very special need for guidance, Pearl withdraws into her "prayer closet" for some intensive prayer: "I have a little private bathroom over there. I lock myself in it and kneel down, and I pray and pray. That room is very special to me!"

Pearl is very emphatic about the power of prayer: "It can move mountains!" At the same time, she says, she never dictates just how each mountain is to be moved.

"I'm not the type to say, 'Lord, I need *this* thing and I'm asking you to do it for me. Or, if I'm in a difficulty, I won't insist, 'I want *this* to be done.' No, I just put the situation to God and ask him to direct me. I pray, 'Lord, if it's your will, then let it be done.'"

Among the many beneficiaries of Pearl's prayers for divine guidance is a young woman who is moving up in her job at a local bank. Her future didn't look so rosy several years ago, when she was a high school student. Her father was sick, both parents were unemployed, and all the family's assets had been wiped out in a hurricane. With five other children to support, the girl's parents could no longer afford to keep her in school. One day they showed up at Poor Relief seeking financial help for their daughter.

"This girl was bright," says Pearl, "and I was really touched by their situation. I asked the couple to wait outside my office and then I prayed and prayed, asking God what to do. All of a sudden it was as if a voice said, *Call Mr. _____ at the bank and ask if he knows anyone who can see the girl through school.* I called. The man's response was immediate: 'I'll ask my club to do it. Just prepare me a report.' By five o'clock I was at the bank with the report, and just a few days later I received the club's first sponsorship check.

"It's funny how things work out," Pearl adds with a chuckle. "That young woman has ended up employed at the very bank where I called for help!"

Pearl's day-in, day-out prayers for direction flow out of her deep conviction of the Lord's care and presence. An experience she had in the early sixties was decisive in this regard.

At the time I was having problems in my life. They weighed on me so much that it was like I was going to break. I didn't know if I could make it. But I kept praying, praying, praying.

One night after going to bed the same as usual, I was suddenly awakened. It seemed to me that I was outside (though I wasn't, really), looking at clouds in the sky. As I watched, the clouds opened and there was Jesus. You've seen pictures that show him revealing his sacred heart? Well, he looked like that, and he seemed to be coming up—out of the earth, out of the grave, I thought. I could even see mud on his robe.

Then Jesus looked at me and raised his right hand in a gesture of blessing. "Be of good courage," he told me. "I will be with you always."

With that, Pearl awoke from her dream—or was it a vision?—and cried out, "I've heard you, Lord!" The experience brought comfort and peace for a time, but as her heavy problems persisted, Pearl found herself sinking back into anxiety. Then again one night she heard the Lord's voice once more, rebuking this time: "Didn't I tell you I would be with you always?" That turned the tide, says Pearl. "From then on, any time I'm getting down—worried and not knowing what to do—I remember Jesus' promise, and then I can release the whole situation into his hands."

So why does Pearline Barrett insist that she "really, really, *really*" believes in prayer? "Because I pray to Someone who has promised to be with me always! That's what keeps me going—in my personal life and on the job. I live on that, you know?"

CHAPTER THREE

Be with Me, Lord, in Time of Need

Biblical Hebrew has a particularly vivid word that captures the mood of the prayers and stories in this chapter. Translated as "cry out," it means both a brief, even wordless, shout of pain and an urgent call for help.

"Crying out" is what the Israelites did when they suffered as slaves in Egypt. It is what the poor and the sick and the helpless and those in danger do in so many of the psalms. It is what the blind beggar Bartimaeus does when he hears that Jesus is walking through Jericho: he "cries out" insistently in the hope that Jesus will hear and heal him (Mark 10:46-52).

Crying out to God lies at the heart of prayer. It recalls the basics about who God is—infinitely merciful—and who we are—desperately needy. Sometimes, after receiving God's help, we forget our neediness for a while. But then along comes another crisis, another cycle of "crying out," another reminder of the reality that without God we are lost.

In this chapter, people from ages eleven to seventy-eight cry out to God from a variety of settings: the slums, a shelter for the homeless, a soup line, a violent neighborhood. Each is in some kind of distress or faces some situation that is beyond their control.

How God will answer those who cry out for help is not

always clear. But Jesus is present with all his followers in every time of need. He understands our cries, having himself prayed "with loud cries and tears" while he was on earth (Hebrews 5:7). Jesus helps us to approach God as he did—crying out with confidence in God's mercy, yet with complete submission to God's will.

Honest prayer helps him thrive in the inner city.

Straight Talk

Look here, Lord.
Things were bad this week in our community.
Someone was shot and killed.
The gun violence keeps increasing.
People are afraid.

Where are you, Lord?
Are you asleep?
I need your help.
You're the one who brought me into this place,
    so this is your problem, too.
Are you going to enlighten me and show me how to
    respond to this?
Are you going to intervene?

What do we do?
What are *you* going to do about this situation?

FATHER DUDLEY ADAMS is mild-mannered, even gentle, in his demeanor, but he is not one to mince words when he prays for help.

No, I talk to the Lord honestly, even kind of rough sometimes. Maybe that's because I love him so much and I know he loves me. I just don't see God as someone with a big stick who will bash me on the nose if I say the wrong thing! Or as some distant Supreme Being who isn't going to want to listen to Dudley Adams. When I pray, I go in with this courage, this confidence that I'm speaking to a loving Friend who will always hear and answer.

After twenty-five years as a Jesuit brother, Dudley Adams decided to become a priest in order to preach the word of God and bring Jesus Christ to people more directly. Ordained in June 1992, Father Adams is carrying out that mission as the pastor of a parish in Kingston's inner city.

What this straight-talking Jesuit usually brings to his Friend's attention in prayers are the sufferings of the people in his Kingston, Jamaica, neighborhood. Many are untrained, unskilled, and therefore unemployable. Many go to bed hungry, just getting by on handouts. Many families are headed by women who, if they find jobs at all, get rock-bottom wages—"not adequate to take care of even one child," says Father Adams. And then there is the violence.

> It certainly has increased recently. Many more people than usual have died violent deaths. Much of it comes down to fighting between gangs who support opposing political parties. This area is rife with gangs, and their style of life is revenge—an eye for an eye. Innocent people get caught in the crossfire. And then, too, you have sporadic robberies. Just last week a businessman was gunned down in broad daylight because he refused to hand over his vehicle to some robbers who were trying to make their escape.

None of his parishioners have been killed, says Father Adams, but many have become fearful and intimidated. When he noticed that Mass attendance was dwindling because of the shooting that seemed to erupt every Sunday morning, Father Adams arranged for police protection at that time. That has helped. But what would help most of all and what he prays for, he says, is "that the good Lord will give the people courage and hope not to be afraid." This is possible, Father Adams knows, because it has happened to him.

> I hear the gunfire. I see the gunmen. It's so close to home, it's not funny! Yes, it's quite a challenge to live in this area. Even if you're very strong-willed, very dedicated and committed, after a while the gun violence gets to you, psychologically, mentally.

In the early stages, I was fearful, living here. But I've asked the Lord to give me courage, and he has. As I see it, I've come here to do God's work, and he's going to let me do it, no matter what else is going on. So I look to God for divine protection in my comings and goings, and somehow I just don't have any fear anymore, not even when I get home late at night.

I'm convinced that Jesus Christ is my guide and my protector. I don't rely on human beings for protection. I rely on Jesus.

That takes faith, and Father Adams seems to have plenty of faith. He also has hope that, with God's help, life in his neighborhood will improve. Seeking to be an instrument for peace and justice, he takes part in many boards and committees, both inside and outside the parish. Concerned about raising the local standard of living, he encourages self-help projects and programs that teach skills by which men and women can learn to support themselves. Political and other divisions in the area make for tricky navigating and slow progress here, but Father Adams gets encouragement to persevere from prayer and Scripture.

This is where I find my consolation, my hope. For example, in the Gospels of Matthew, Mark, and Luke, I see Jesus involved in so many delicate situations and political controversies and confrontations. I see him overcoming the antagonism of some people, persevering with his work despite the opposition of others who try to block and trap him. "Look at what Jesus did," I tell myself. "Try to imitate him. He's with you to help you." And each day as I go about my work, I ask myself, "How would Jesus handle this? What does he want me to do in this situation?"

The psalms, too, are a support and model for me. There's a lot of saying, "Look here, God, you have to help me!" They're real and honest prayers that give me the courage and desire to stay close to God and keep working despite obstacles.

And, of course, there's the Mass. I thrive on it. Celebrating Mass every day is at the heart of everything. This is where I get my food, hope, inspiration, strength to carry on in this volatile environment.

Commitment to do God's will in the place where God has called him is what characterizes Father Adams in another moment of prayer to his beloved Friend:

> To you, O Lord,
> I entrust all my hopes,
>   all my trials and miseries.
> May all my actions be ordered and disposed
>   according to your will.
> As I toil for peace and unity in your vineyard,
>   make me strong and faithful
>   to praise you evermore.
> And may nothing ever cloud my conscience
>   or hinder my progress
>   until the day of Jesus comes. Amen.

Poor widow in the poorest country in the hemisphere, Lourdie Sanon faces the challenge of caring for her five children only through her lifeline to the Lord.

A persistent widow pleads her cause.

It's Me Again, Lord

"DEFENDER OF WIDOWS" is an Old Testament description of God that highlights God's concern for the neediest and least protected members of society.

Thirty-two-year-old Lourdie Sanon of Port-au-Prince, Haiti, may not be familiar with this title of God's, but she has experienced the truth of it every day since the traffic accident that killed her husband about two years ago. Though tears may come to Lourdie's eyes as she describes the struggles of caring for her five children, this young mother knows prayer as a lifeline to a God who hears and helps—for example, by restoring health to the son mentioned in the following prayer.

It's me again, Lord.

I know I call on you all the time, but who else can I talk to? Who else will help me? Who else sees?

You are the only one who knows.

I see other women with their husbands, and I feel lonely sometimes.

I feel that I'm very young to have five children and nobody to help me out with them.

Well, that's not quite true. I'm grateful that my brother-in-law comes by to give me something sometimes. And that my aunt has taken us in for a while.

But Lord, I'm afraid they'll get tired of us and won't want to help anymore. Even if it's family, you can't live off other people forever.

You are the only one who knows.

And Lord, I don't know what to do with these kids.

They are hungry sometimes, and I have nothing to feed them. I can't send them to school. I can't provide for them, because I can't find any work.

And now my oldest son is sick—so sick, with a high fever every night. The doctor prescribed some medicine, but you know I have no money to buy it.

God, my son has no father but you. You gave me this child and you are able to heal him. Lord, I love my son. Please save him.

You are the only one who knows.

Thank you, Lord, that I can turn to you with my problems and that you are always with me.

If I didn't have you, I could never find the strength even to get up in the morning. But you help me out.

I have nothing on my own, but you provide everything, Lord.

Because of that, every day is like a miracle to me.

struggle to provide and survive, Jean-Hubert and Moïse might be expected to display at least a touch of bitterness or self-pity. Instead they demonstrate a touching concern for other family members and an uncomplicated trust in God. *Bondye*, they call him in their native Creole—"good God."

"What do you say to God when you pray?"

Jean-Hubert fidgets with his neon green plastic sandals, reflecting. His younger brother jumps in: "When I pray, I ask *Bondye* to help my parents and give them courage to keep going." Jean-Hubert nods slowly in agreement. Yes, that is the first thing he prays for too. "Because my parents are very poor," he explains. "I ask *Bondye* to make me strong so that I can keep going to school, so that when I'm older I can help my parents to have a better life. I ask him to help me learn so that I can become something tomorrow."

Less than half of Haitian children attend school. Moïse and Jean-Hubert are in that minority—when their parents can afford to send them. Not that the school, which is run by Catholic nuns, is expensive. It's just that you need shoes to go to school. And when you can barely scrape together enough money for food and shelter, shoes become a luxury you can't afford.

So Jean-Hubert and Moïse discuss this particular need earnestly and often with their heavenly Father. "When school opened this year, I couldn't go because I didn't have any shoes," says Jean-Hubert. "I knew that my mother didn't have any money to buy them for me either. But I really wanted to go to school, so I prayed that *Bondye* would find me a way to get some shoes." He did, through the nuns who gave Jean-Hubert some money for his purchase. "When I got my sneakers I was so happy! Thank you, *Bondye!*"

Now it is Moïse who has outgrown his shoes and who is praying for new ones with the expectation born of many such answers to prayer. His approach is straightforward, trusting: "If I need something I just ask *Bondye* and he helps me. He always gives me what I need."

"When do you talk to God during the day?"

At various moments, as needs arise. At the regular times of prayer in the school chapel. At church every Sunday. And especially at night before going to sleep, the boys explain.

Every night Moïse kneels down in a corner of the shanty where he lives, in front of the picture of Jesus that is tacked to the wall, to pray ten Hail Marys. "I say to *Bondye*, 'My night is in your hands.'" Stretched out on the bed he shares with other siblings, Jean-Hubert likes to silently review the Ten Commandments. "I ask *Bondye* to forgive all my sins, and I ask him to protect my life."

Even amidst the clatter of the cooking pots being scrubbed at high noon in the soup kitchen courtyard, it's easy to picture these brothers entrusting themselves to God in the stillness of the night, here in this country where life seems so fragile, so vulnerable. They entrust others to his care, too. A sister too sick to get up. A brother and a cousin who have died—"I pray *Bondye* to open the door of heaven for them," says Jean-Hubert.

A couple of fluffy chicks run by, pecking up the grains of rice that have fallen from the servers' ladles. Time for Moïse and Jean-Hubert to collect their family's share. They pick up their containers and walk back to the line, past the burlap sacks of spinach and eggplant that will be on tomorrow's menu, past the scurrying chicks that will also end up on the Pétion family dinner table one day.

"If I didn't have *Bondye* in my life, I wouldn't have faith that things will get better," says Jean-Hubert. He is concerned about the future, of course. Would anyone look forward to hunger, or to a lifetime of standing in soup lines?

There is no way for Jean-Hubert—or anyone else, for that matter—to know what the future holds. But for this young man in the torn shirt, there is this heartening reality: he does not face it alone. "I know *Bondye,* and he always takes care of me."

> **Good Father, *Bondye,***
>   **my life is in your hands.**
> **Open the door of heaven**
>   **to provide what I need today.**
> **Even before my prayer is on my lips,**
> **you know what it will be—**
>   **for shoes…**
>   **a decent job…**
>   **protection…**
>   **help for those I love…**
>   **hope for the future.**
> **Take care of me again today**
>   **and keep me very close to you,**
>   **so that one day**
> **I may see you open the door of heaven**
>   **to welcome me home.**

"I couldn't hang on if I didn't pray," says Sister Rocío Pérez. This nun from Colombia has given many years of service in Cuba, Mexico, the Dominican Republic, and now Haiti. "Coming here was a bit difficult at first because I didn't speak French or Creole," she says. "But the students helped me, and I learned little by little."

"Where are you, Lord? You see all the misery that people are in."

Misery and Mystery

THE SOUNDS AND SMELLS of Cité Soleil, Haiti's worst slum, drift in through the open window of Sister Rocío Pérez's office. Roosters crow, mangy dogs bark, pigs grunt their way through mounds of rotting garbage, children shriek, vendors offer their wares, the occasional vehicle honks and brakes as it tries to navigate the crowded corridors that pass for streets here.

The Don Bosco Center, where Sister Rocío and her Salesian sisters live and run a training school for illiterate young women, is an oasis of peace amid this crowded shantytown's noise and squalor. The sisters try hard to keep it that way: for many of their students, the school provides the only peace and order they will ever know.

Sister Rocío, a soft-spoken woman with a shy smile, is distressed this morning. She has just learned that one of her students has died. "Of a fever, I think. Maybe I could have done something to help. But no one told me." Her careworn face becomes animated as she describes the dangers and hardships that her students face in their Cité Soleil homes.

"There are robbers. There are pimps. There are mothers who push their daughters into prostitution so that they can bring home a little money. Some of our girls are in physical danger. Right now one is being followed around by a tramp who wants to move in with her. She's scared to death that he'll find out where she lives and break in some night. She's by herself, in a rented room with flimsy locks." Sister Rocío pauses, considering the girl's dilemma. "We can't run a boarding school here, but I think we'll have to take her in with us somehow."

Clearly, Sister Rocío's heart is with her girls. And, good mother that she is, her prayer is one continuous, fervent petition for their well-being.

No matter where I begin, my prayer always centers around the girls. I think about them first thing when I wake up, and all through the day I'm bringing their needs to the Lord. Maybe I talk too much when I pray, I don't know. I do find it difficult to enter into that silence where you can hear God's voice. But I know God is with me even when I can't quiet my mind. He knows what I'm made of. He understands that I get easily distracted, preoccupied....

And have you seen the houses where these girls live? You can't imagine.

But just getting to the Don Bosco Center—going into a tiny part of this twenty-seven-square-mile slum—stimulates a visitor's imagination. It's a sea of shanties made of tin and cardboard and wood scraps and sometimes cinderblocks—jammed together, tilting precariously, looking as if any good gust of wind might knock them down. No bigger than an average walk-in closet, most of them, and each one housing five, eight, ten people. No garbage collection here. No electricity—except what is siphoned off illegally. Fetid water stands in the drainage ditches running right by the hovels. No plumbing here either.

It poured last night, and the gray mud of Cité Soleil is slimy underfoot. Those drainage ditches overflowed again, spilling raw sewage everywhere, Sister Rocío explains. "The water came up to there." She points to a spot in the middle of the school's courtyard. And, as usual, it flooded into the shanties.

"People here suffer terribly during the heavy rains. Nobody

can sleep. If they have a bed, they put the children on it. The rest of the family has to stand until daybreak, when it usually stops raining and they can begin bailing out." The damp, unsanitary conditions breed all kinds of diseases and ailments—malaria, tuberculosis, rheumatism, typhoid.

"Many of our girls, when they get sick, have nothing: no one to take care of them, no little corner where they can lie down and be pampered a bit." Sister Rocío's eyes fill with tears. Perhaps she is thinking of the student who just died, unnoticed and unhelped.

> I struggle with all this sometimes. I know that God is all-powerful and all-loving. But sometimes I ask him, "Where are you, Lord? You see all the misery that people are in. And so many are crying out to you, praying and fasting. But still we wait and we don't see you. Where are you?"
>
> Really, though, I do know that God is here, sustaining us daily in so many ordinary-looking ways. Often I don't see him because I'm looking for the wrong thing—some dramatic intervention, some spectacular miracle or instant solution. But God is present everywhere and, in a special way, in the worst poverty. And so I see all my girls and their families caught up in a great mystery: misery, suffering, abandonment. And God is there.... God is there.

Sister Rocío is not romanticizing poverty. She knows it too well for that. But as she struggles with the misery around her, neither does she question God's love and power; she knows God too well for that. Somehow, without her fully understanding them or being able to reconcile them, the two realities find a place in her heart. And from that place of pondering and trusting springs the motherly intercession that is Sister Rocío's prayer.

Why, O Lord, do you stand far off?
Why do you hide yourself in times of trouble?

Rise up, O Lord; O God, lift up your hand;
do not forget the oppressed.

But you do see! Indeed you note
trouble and grief,
that you may take it into your hands;
the helpless commit themselves to you;
you have been the helper of the orphan.

O Lord, you will hear the desire of the meek;
you will strengthen their heart,
you will incline your ear
to do justice for the orphan and the oppressed.

PSALMS 10:1, 12, 14, 17-18

*"I never dreamed of retiring to a
shelter for the homeless."*

Homeless in the Golden Years

LEANING ON HER WALKING STICK, gripping the plastic bags
that hold her possessions, seventy-eight-year-old Mabel Ward
comes slowly across the room toward you. Her legs must be
bothering her today; they often do since that stroke she had in
1990. But Peter Simpson, Mabel's junior by six years, has
noticed. With a courtly flourish, he rises, offers an arm, and
steers her to a nearby bench.

Mabel eases herself down and turns to you with a soulful
look. "I never thought things would turn out like this," she
says. She pulls out a worn beige handkerchief and dabs at her
eyes.

The situation that has taken Mabel by surprise is the fact
that in these last years of her life she has no home, no family,
and no means of support. That's a bitter pill for someone who
has been "a hardworking woman" all her life and who even
now aspires to get strong enough to "do a day's work and earn
a few dollars." Her family has died out, Mabel explains, and
there is no one left to help her. Kicked out of the house, she
lived on the streets of Kingston until some church members
discovered her plight and brought her to the government-run
shelter for the homeless where you sit talking.

Mabel's tears keep falling and Peter pats her shoulder in an
awkward yet tender gesture of consolation. "Don't cry,
Mabel. It's all right," he says comfortingly. "Don't forget the
Lord. God is with you. And you know he'll always take care of
you."

Coming as they do from a fellow resident of the shelter,
from someone who has also known abandonment and hard-

A study in dignity in the face of adversity, Mabel Ward and Peter Simpson are residents of a Kingston, Jamaica, shelter for the homeless.

ship, Peter's simple words strike home. These are not unfounded hopes that he is offering Mabel: here are tried and tested truths that have carried Peter through many a hard time.

Peter is not a man of many words, and of his struggles he says simply, "Oh, I've had my ups and downs." He would rather tell you about how God has taken care of him. "Whenever I have a problem, I pray and God solves it. If I'm hungry today, I won't be hungry tomorrow, because I'll pray and God will provide even more food than I need." Lately, he says, the Lord has provided some part-time employment: "I asked God to help me find work, and now I've got a painting job I really like."

Mabel has dried her tears and begins to offer her own reflections about prayer and God's faithfulness. Distressed though she may be at times, she is a woman of faith who turns to God often and talks to him unaffectedly, "like I talk to a natural man." At night when everything is quiet in the shelter, she likes to lie in her bed and think about God. That's when she "meditates," Mabel tells you—and because her strong Jamaican accent makes it hard for you to grasp everything she is saying, Peter jumps in to explain what she means by meditation: "You go deep down. You go quietly. You pray in your mind and your heart."

Because Peter and Mabel are pressed on every side by urgent practical needs, you are struck by the fact that their prayer seems to include contemplation as well as petition. Their need for the gifts of life does not cloud their ability to enjoy the Giver. *If I were in their shoes, would I be too preoccupied by my problems to talk to God about anything else?* you wonder. Neither do their own needs make them insensitive to others, you discover when you ask Peter what sorts of things he prays for.

"I pray for other people. I pray for the woman who runs this shelter—she's such a good woman. I pray for this lady here." He nods toward Mabel. And with a disarming smile, he adds an intention that will hearten you long after you have taken leave of this homeless couple: "Well, I've met you today, and so now I'll always pray for *you!*"

Lord, thank you for Mabel and Peter.
I'm grateful that you brought us together
and that you were there with us as we met.

I'm grateful that you gave me a glimpse
into some of the things that you must love
    about this woman and this man.
Help me to imitate those things.

Let me be more like Mabel, Lord:
open to hearing the truth about your unfailing care
    and mercy—even when I don't feel your presence,
    even when I'm deeply distressed.
You know that I'm not always very open to being
    encouraged.
Sometimes I want to wallow in the blues.
Help me to change, to hope in your love.

And at night, on my bed at home,
    may I remember Mabel lying in the shelter,
    thinking of you.
May more and more nights find me meditating—
"going quietly, deep down" into mind and heart
like her.

CHAPTER FOUR

It Is Good to Give Thanks to You, Lord

Various writers on prayer have observed that we most often address God—whether in the Bible or in our own lives—in one of two ways: with pleas or thanksgiving, with petition or praise. It is in these moments, one writer maintains, that "one is at the heart of prayer." The preceding chapter, with its cries to God for help, presents one side of the pendulum swing; this chapter offers expressions of the gratitude that characterizes the other.

These sharings reflect the blessed moments or seasons in a person's spiritual life when feelings of thankfulness predominate, when distress—though perhaps not absent—is not felt acutely enough to push cries of pain to the forefront.

It is easy to relate to some of the reasons that people in this chapter give for being grateful to God. God's love and presence, answered prayer, skills of various kinds, the marvels of nature, a child's success in school, the privilege of helping others, a comfortable bed, a loving family—all this we can understand.

Harder to fathom is how some of these people, given their lot in life, can experience any gratitude at all. Yet a single mother raising her children in a slum is passionately grateful to Jesus for giving her a second chance to follow him. A poor, bedridden woman's eyes shine as she declares that God does "everything" for her.

Such examples seem to indicate that the two extremes of the pendulum swing can work together. Times of distress, weathered with God's grace, can make for a clearer vision of God's presence and faithfulness, and thus for the heartfelt thanks to which we are all called: "Give thanks in all circumstances; for this is the will of God in Christ Jesus for you" (1 Thessalonians 5:18).

Everything to Be Thankful For

TAKE A RIGHT AFTER YOU WALK into the main door of the clinic. Go down the hall, past the benches where the outpatients are waiting to be treated, and look left, over the halfwall, into the women's ward. There, sitting in her bed in the left-hand corner of the light and airy room is Simone Gustave, an eight-year resident of the clinic.

Treatment has halted the progress of Hansen's disease (leprosy) in Simone, but no medicine or therapy can reverse its effects; she is too disabled to live on her own. Don't let that fool you, though. Here is a woman with plenty of spunk, vigor, and persuasive powers. Whether or not you speak Creole, you will probably not emerge from an encounter with Simone without having bought one of the items she crochets!

**Here I sit, propped up with pillows on my bed
in the corner of the ward,
my home for eight years now.**

**What do I do here all day?
Someone asked me that this afternoon.
Maybe they think I get bored or lonely.
But how could I,
when you are here with me, Lord?**

**You are my life and you give me everything.
The light that streams in from the window behind me,
the flowers on my nightstand,
the wheelchair by my bed and the special shoes
    that help me to get around,**

Simone Gustave has offered up many prayers here in her nook of the Cardinal Léger Clinic for victims of Hansen's disease, in Léogane, Haiti. Simone never learned some details such as when she was born (sometime between 1930 and 1941, she thinks, when Stenio Joseph Vincent was president of Haiti). But she has a grip on life's basics—God's nearness and love.

the skill to crochet my doilies and table runners
  (and, by the way, please let that broken bone in my
  arm heal quickly so I can use my crochet hook again),
the nuns and doctors and nurses who take care of me—
all this comes from you, good Lord.

And so with you I sing.
I pray.
I talk to my neighbors.
I watch the people passing in the corridor.

Sometimes my son is there, coming to visit me.
Sometimes I spot groups of visitors who come to see the
  clinic.
I always try to sell them my doilies.
I drive a hard bargain, too.
Sometimes I see the outpatients who have come for
  treatment—
  the sad mother with the white spots of leprosy on her
  knuckles and her little girl in hand,
  young men in wheelchairs,
  so many who need your help.
So as I sit here I ask you:
Bless them all, good Lord.

I pray for all my brothers and sisters,
  for those in Haiti
  and those in all other countries.
I pray for the people who have helped me by helping this
  clinic. It's because of them that I can be here.

Keep watching over Simone Gustave, Lord.
Keep her strong.
Give her courage.

Mother Mary, pray for me.
Holy Spirit, direct me and watch over me.
 Bless me and purify me.

Thank you, God.
You do all this for Simone Gustave.

"What good is life?" the young woman wrote.
"I'm going nowhere. I'd rather be dead."

Alice on My Mind
By Sister Anne Marie

THE WOMAN WHO FOUNDED THE RELIGIOUS ORDER I belong to was a godly soul with a simple way of praying. She especially liked to pray in church, but she couldn't get there as often as she wanted because she lived in the country. So during the day she would climb up to her attic, look out the window toward the distant steeple, and think of Jesus in the tabernacle there. Her prayer was simply, "Jesus, I adore you and I love you."

Well, my prayer is simple too. Every morning I go to the chapel and tell the Lord, "Here I am, the empty-headed one who never has much to say. But you know how grateful I am to you, how much I love you, and how much more I want to love you. Read all that is in my heart, Lord."

And he does. I've never heard his voice in an audible way, never had a mystical revelation or anything like that. But what Jesus has given me is a deep inner peace, a sense of his presence that never leaves me. I have to say that I always feel joyful at heart. And in my forty-five years as a nun, I can't remember a single day when I regretted entering the religious life.

Not that there haven't been difficult moments right from the beginning. For example, in choosing this way of life I had to go against the wishes of my parents. You see, I was brought up in a fairly well-to-do family, and the religious order into which God called me has a special concern for the poor. In my country, we work in areas where the people are desperately poor in every way. Perhaps the contrast was too shocking for my parents. I remember that a few days after I entered the order, my mother came to see how I was doing. She looked around and then said to me: "So you

Sister Anne Marie seeks to live a hidden life of service to God and his poor. Her prayers of praise and thanksgiving rise up to the Lord from this convent chapel in Haiti.

prefer this to what you grew up with? I don't understand you. People always tend towards what is more beautiful, but you have chosen to go down into the pit."

What could I say? Because it is hard to explain. It's a call from God, a special grace. Why else would I feel most at home, most at ease, most myself, whenever I'm with the poor children I've been teaching?

My parents may not have supported my decision at first, but they were very good people who had a great influence on my spiritual life. My mother was a woman of faith, always ready with an inspiring proverb. My father was a wonderful man—loving, generous, a model husband and father. I had a very affectionate relationship with him, and I think this is why my relationship with God is so trusting and affectionate as well; I simply transferred what I felt for my father to God the Father.

As a result, with my Father I have a relaxed, joyful, intimate relationship. I'm happy just to love him and to know that he loves me. When I run into trouble, I tell him very simply, "Lord, I know you've allowed this for some reason, and I know you love me—so I know you'll get me out of this!" And he always does. In fact, he's excessively generous with me; he spoils me, going beyond my expectations to give me my heart's desires.

Here's just one example. One day I received a letter from a former student I'll call Alice. She had come to us as a five-year-old orphan, and we had given her a home and an education and found her a job. Now Alice was thirty and living in the United States. Her letter was a cry of anguish.

"What good is my life?" she wrote me. "I'm not called to be a nun, I'm not married, and I'm getting older. I'm going nowhere. All I do is get up, go to work, go to bed, get up, go to work, go to bed. I'd rather be dead than live like this."

Reading between the lines I could tell that what Alice wanted more than anything was a husband with whom to create a good

Christian home. And I sensed that this is what God wanted for her, too.

I was teaching a class of older girls at the time, and I recruited them as my prayer partners. Without giving them Alice's name or whereabouts, I told them her story: "Here's an orphan, someone who has no one to love her and no one to love. We're going to pray that God puts a good husband on her path." Being nineteen, the girls were very happy to pray for this! I wrote back to Alice and suggested that she get away for a while and spend her Christmas vacation with another former student, who was married and living in Italy.

Meanwhile, my students and I went into the chapel every day to pray that the Lord would give Alice a life companion who would love and understand her. We kept this up faithfully for about two months.

Alice took my advice and went to Italy for Christmas. And whom do you think she met while she was there? A friend of the family she was visiting—an Italian who fell in love with her and proposed by the end of her visit. "Listen, how can I marry you when I hardly know you?" Alice told him. "But if you're really serious about this, write to the one person in this world who cares about me and tell her what your intentions are."

And so one day I received a letter from a thirty-five-year-old Italian, explaining why he felt that Alice was the woman for him. "Give it more time," I wrote back and, to make a long story short, after a long-distance courtship Alice and her Italian friend were married. Today, after fifteen years of marriage, they are still very happy and are raising their two children to follow the Lord.

Of course, the girls were delighted when I told them what had happened. And Alice, who knew that they had been praying for her, sent me a hundred dollars so that we could have our own little party to celebrate her wedding day. For all of us, Alice's story was a lesson about faith, prayer, and God's desire to give us joy when we ask him for it.

Sometimes when I'm sitting quietly in the chapel, I remember Alice—and so many other people for whom I've seen the Lord do wonderful things. My head may be empty of fine words with which to express my thanks, but my heart is filled with love and gratitude as I reflect on God's tender mercy.

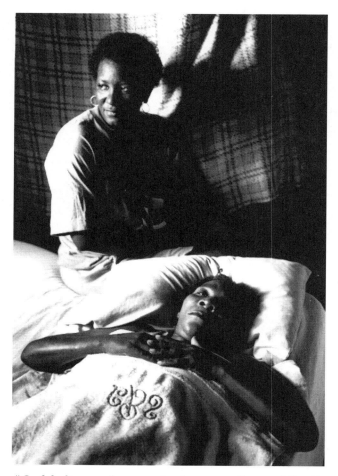

"God helps me because he loves me," says Minette Sappleton, tended here by daughter Paulette. Minette has spent most of the past fifteen years in bed but is grateful that God does "everything" for her.

have a pain in my head or my feet, I pray, and then I revive; the pain goes away. So I know God is listening to me when I talk to him. He helps me because he loves me.

You seem very certain about God's love for you, Minette.
I am! I know that God loves me so much. I'm getting all the love I want from Jesus Christ. All the love. I couldn't want any better love than I'm getting already from my family and from the Lord. God is like a husband to me.

Is there anything else you like to say to the Lord?
Well, I thank him all the time for everything. For his love. For how he always answers my prayer. (Sometimes it takes a long time, but he always answers!) For giving me good encouragement every day. I don't know how I would have managed if I didn't have the Lord.

Lying down here for fifteen years is not easy. But I know God is with me. He is with me all the while, night and day. He is not leaving me, that I know.

So you see, God is good, and God is great, and God does everything for me. And that is why I thank him.

The son and grandson of missionaries, Pastor Wallace Turnbull has spent most of his seventy years serving Haiti's rural dwellers. Terraced fields in the background demonstrate his commitment to improving their material as well as their spiritual condition.

peasants would stop by to bring us a gift of food. We didn't tell them we were broke, but the Lord did and they responded.

So this life of faith is something that is natural to us. We've prayed constantly all our lives and feel God's hand upon us. We rely on God to provide everything we need—including wisdom about how to use each day for his glory.

I thank the Lord for some dramatic answers to our prayers.

I remember one period when we were working very hard to build up congregations in the countryside, especially in the northwest of Haiti. This was a very difficult area to penetrate: we had to go into a town by jeep and then take off on horseback or on foot to these remote outposts where people were being converted from voodoo. Each of these congregations needed a church, and we were struggling to get materials. So Eleanor and I decided to ask God for a chunk of money. Up till then we hadn't received such large gifts, but we decided to dream big. "Lord," we prayed, "if we had $10,000, we'd be able to build a couple of churches." And what should come in the mail right after that but a check for $10,000! Now we're responsible for over three hundred churches extending north and northwest into the country from our mission here in Fermathe. About one hundred thousand people attend those churches every Sunday—quite a change from our first service, when only three people came!

I thank the Lord for showing us how to provide educational opportunities for Haitian children and young people. We have a network of over 280 primary schools and run a high school and vocational training center. But it started slowly, with a little box of a building I made that still stands down the road.

At the time we arrived in Haiti, only 2 percent of the population could read. In all these mountains we found only two young men who were literate—and only at second grade level. We hired them to teach the little they knew. Now we have a number of university graduates in this area, and young people who work in various professions. But the need remains great: in three out of four cases, country children do not get to attend school.

I thank the Lord for help in meeting people's desperate need for medical care. If you look around here at the Mission, you'll see a comprehensive medical ministry staffed by Haitian doctors and nurses. It includes two hospitals, a medical and a dental clinic, and public health teams that travel into remote areas.

And when I think of how it all started: with Eleanor's mother—"Granny," as people came to call her—sitting on her front steps with a box of medical supplies and ministering to people's needs as best she could. It was simple treatment, but people were grateful because it was all they had. We began giving worm medicine and people would come back to thank us and show the result wrapped up in a banana leaf: half a gallon or so of ascarid worms that they had passed. They look like night crawlers, and eventually they affect the brain. In this area, people still die of worms.

Eleanor carried sick people to the university hospital in Port-au-Prince in those early days. Finally one of the doctors told her, "Madame Wallace, we can't care for all these people. But if you keep patients up at your place, we will prescribe medication." So we bought six little metal cots, and six pneumonia patients moved into them one winter. That's what started our hospital.

We certainly didn't know what to do to meet people's medical needs, but through prayer the Lord gave us ideas and guided us step by step. I'm so grateful he did—and does.

I thank the Lord for being with us in the difficult moments—and they have been many. The Lord never said that Christians would be exempt from difficulties! We're normal people with weaknesses.

"God blesses me with so much."

What Hard Life?

IT'S A MUGGY FRIDAY IN JUNE in Riverton City, Jamaica. Beverley Moore, forty, is sitting on her porch doing the family laundry in a metal washtub. This day began early for her, with a 4:30 A.M. trip to the food market where she buys the produce that she resells. The small profit goes toward supporting herself, her nine children, and her mother, who lives with the family.

A single mother scrabbling from dawn to dusk to keep her family clean and fed, Beverley might be described as having a hard life. But that's not how she sees it.

> Listen, when you know God, you don't talk about a hard life. You have a God who provides. To others it looks hard, but it looks easy to me because I don't watch what is hard. I watch the Creator and what he can do for me.
>
> So you don't worry about tomorrow. You think about God. You know that he is your provider, your source of living. So when you wake up tomorrow, you have your source. He is your source, he is your husband. So you don't have a problem, because your husband must provide for you. And he will. He says he will take care of you; and what he says, he will do.

Some of Beverley's children have gathered on the porch, listening to what their mother has to say about this provider God. She becomes animated, something of a fiery preacher, as she describes what he is like. "A supernatural, miraculous, superstar God! An all-purpose God who circles all around to give you everything!" God knows everything and can do everything, she insists. At the same time, "he won't push anything on you."

You have to ask God for what you need. And you have to believe. Not just say it with your mouth and your tongue. You must believe from the depth of your heart that he can carry you through the dungeon and the fire. You have to really believe what God and the Bible say, and then he brings miracles alive for you.

Beverley's mother is on the porch, too, cradling one of her younger grandchildren. Washtub shoved aside, Beverley is explaining how the Bible is God's living word to her, nourishing her faith and speaking to her especially through the stories and statements of other people who cried out to God.

I like to meditate upon the psalms, you know? The parts about deliverance, being in trouble, bringing the help, God guiding and protecting you—all those things. The psalms of David going through distress: when he has needs, he calls upon God and God helps him.

That shows you that you can do the same thing. We can hear from the same God. He's not a dead God! He's right beside us in everything, and he understands us supernaturally. Mighty God!

Assured that she has God's ear, Beverley whispers into it freely: "at home, at church, on the bus, right here when I wash clothes—anywhere, I pray. Just talk to God silent and he understands everything, every little grunt. He's that kind of a God."

He answers her prayers, too, says Beverley, working "miracles too many to tell." For example, as often happens, on this very morning she had walked to the market in faith, with no money in her pocket. "On the way, I said, 'God, I don't have one cent to my name!'" And Beverley's "all-purpose God" worked things out for her, moving some of the vendors to let her take produce on credit. "God helped me to sell it and so I was able to pay the people back and make a little something to take home."

It's windy on the porch, and Beverley tightens the olive green kerchief that covers her hair. "You know," she reflects, "God blesses me with so much that I don't even understand it." Her eyes fill with tears. "Sometimes I say, 'God, when can I do something for *you?*'"

One little thing I can do: when I pray, first I always give thanks for everything. I thank God for keeping me, for carrying me, for everything he is doing for me. I thank him for the food he has provided, for the clothes, for these children. Yeah man, I thank him because he's the one who has given me everything! So I thank him for the great and for the small.

Topping Beverley's list of things to be grateful for is the gift of God's love and salvation. Earlier in her life, when her two oldest children were born, Beverley was close to the Lord. "But then I fell away and lived out of God for ten long years."

But God sent people to warn me: "Bev, turn your life back to God!" I told them, "Soon come," but every time another pressure came to keep me away. But God saw my soul and he talked to me. One night he called me by name: "Bev, Bev, why are you so wicked to yourself?" And then I knew I had to respect and worship him again. Because I had nothing any more and I could see a starvation coming upon me.

So I made up my mind to come back to Jesus a second time and stay with him. Nothing tripped me up this time, nothing held me back. Nothing, nothing, nothing! Breathless I ran, breathless I came back to Jesus.

So you see, I love God and I have to give him thanks, because

I know he loves me. He could have let me die during those ten years. I see some others dead with no second chance like me. Dead, dead, dead! Why did I have a second chance with God and not them? Why was I able to make it up with God before my time had come?

Beverley doesn't have answers to these questions. But she is very clear about the thanksgiving she wants to offer: "Love God, thank him, worship him. And above all, keep my body as a living sacrifice, holy and clean, so God can use me as his servant. I must live holy to almighty God!"

Words of insight and wisdom from a garbage dump shanty-town, where a woman with a scrubboard wrestles to keep clothing, mind, and body as clean as she possibly can, for Jesus' sake.

CHAPTER FIVE

Lord, How Great Are Your Works!

A dying baby. A counselor working with a drug addict. A mother too poor to feed her children. A preacher with a debilitating back injury. A young couple who cannot afford a wedding. These are some of the urgent situations recounted in this chapter—stories of God's intervention in answer to prayer to meet a special need.

And here are answers like those we so often dream of when we send up our prayer petitions. People are healed. Lives are turned around. Food or money or whatever else is needed appears. These are the obvious saving acts of God, the providential rescues that we are aware of (as opposed to the more hidden workings by which God acts on our behalf and sustains our very existence).

Like the "saving deeds" of God recounted in Scripture, such interventions support our faith by what they reveal about God. He is a God of miracles, with power to intervene in the natural order. He is the master orchestrator, also working through all kinds of natural factors so that a person or object materializes on the scene to meet a critical need at just the right moment. He is a loving God, who takes note of even the smallest details of our lives and who is ready to intervene in answer to our prayers whenever these prayers are truly in our best interest—which God alone knows.

Seeing God's powerful love at work moved the composers of the psalms to cries of praise more than two thousand years ago. That response of praise remains fitting as we contemplate God's saving deeds—in small matters and great—in our lives today. "How great are your works, O Lord!" (Psalms 92:6). "O Lord God of hosts, who is as mighty as you, O Lord?" (Psalms 89:9).

"Please come and pray. Our child is dying."

God Has Always Come Through

REVEREND HUGH SHERLOCK USHERS YOU WARMLY into the living room of his home, where photos, awards, and other mementos hint at the life of service he has led. There are reminders of the national and international positions he has held in the Methodist Church. There is a copy of the Jamaican national anthem, whose words he penned ("every line is a prayer"). There is a plaque honoring him as the founder of Boystown, an outreach which includes two schools serving some eight hundred children, as well as associations and training programs for many other young people. Reverend Sherlock launched Boystown in 1940 by playing an informal game of cricket with a bunch of at-risk kids in a rough West Kingston neighborhood.

The remarkable development of Boystown over the years is one of many undertakings whose success Reverend Sherlock attributes to prayer. "Not so much prayer in the formal way," he explains. "What I do is get into a contemplative mood and think about God. As I meditate, I seem to get nearer to God and I communicate with him. I feel that he's hearing me, showing me the way forward. If I'm praying for a certain project, vision comes, and with it confidence that God is guiding and will provide the resources."

As Reverend Sherlock recounts experiences from a lifetime of prayer, you are struck not only by his impressive recall but also by his sense of wonder at how God intervenes in human lives: "I've taken the most tremendous risks, but God has always come through!"

The following story is one example among many.

Listening to Reverend Hugh Sherlock, an hour passes quickly. An accomplished storyteller, Reverend Sherlock draws on a large stock of personal experiences from his many years as a minister of the Methodist Church.

My first experience as a minister of the Methodist Church was to be sent into exile—at least that's what it felt like at the time! I was assigned to the Turks and Caicos, a poor and lonely group of islands at the southeast end of the Bahamas. Getting to my post was rough; you had to cross a very nasty channel where the Atlantic and the Caribbean meet. And once there you felt very isolated. But it was a good training ground, a place to discover whether or not you had the gifts of ministry.

I learned many valuable lessons during that time, but one thing that I didn't discover until I went back to Turks for a visit some years later was that the people had given me a name: "the healer," they called me. When I questioned them about this, they said, "It's because your prayers for healing for so many people were answered." In fact, there had been a number of incidents where I had seen God heal. One I recall particularly....

Early one morning there came a knock at my door. I went out and saw a young man standing there. "Reverend," he said, "my child is very sick. The doctor has come to examine him and he says there is no hope of saving him. He is very sorry but there is nothing he can do." The young father paused and looked expectantly at me. "Please come to our home and pray with us for our child's life."

I accepted the invitation, and we set out together. On the way, though, I made a quick stop at Florence Barrow's. Aunt Flo, as everyone called her, was a saintly eighty-year-old member of our church. Standing at her gate, I told her where I was going and asked for her help: "Please begin praying as of right now, so that our prayers may unite and this child be spared!" Aunt Flo immediately went into her room to pray.

Arriving at the young man's house, I was shown a child of about two who was very sick indeed. In fact, he seemed to have fallen into a coma. "The doctor says his situation is hopeless," the tired mother told me.

"Well, what about you? Do you think there is hope?" I asked her.

"Yes, I do," she replied. "That's why we sent for you."

I took the little boy's hand and together with his parents began to offer prayer. Our petition was urgent but very simple: "God, please give healing to this child. Lead him to a complete recovery of health and strength." I returned to the mission house without having seen any change in the boy's condition but feeling that we had done what we were supposed to do.

I was getting on with some desk work when there came another knock on the door. It was the boy's father again, but what a different expression he wore. He was smiling, laughing, beside himself with joy. "Father, the child has changed! He's out of the coma! He's talking, he's clapping. He wants some food, he wants some milk." It was true: the boy was indeed on the road to recovery, and how we rejoiced—his family and Aunt Flo and I—to see what God had done.

One day twelve years after returning to Jamaica, I had occasion to experience that joy and awe once again. I was back in Turks for a short visit, leading the cricket team I had formed at Boystown. One of my former students from Turks had started a team and challenged us to a match.

The morning of the match, I walked out of the house where I was staying and found a fine-looking young chap waiting for me.

"Hello, Reverend Sherlock," he said. "I've come to show you across to the cricket field and to carry your bat for you." He seemed so friendly, so eager to do this little service for me. And when he identified himself, I found out why. "I'm the boy you prayed for twelve years ago. I've been fit and healthy ever since!"

Praise God, the real Healer, who gives us the privilege of sharing in his work!

*"Almighty God… it's time for you and me
to have a little talk again."*

Staying Rightside Up in
Upside-Down Times

ASKING FLORETTA THOMPSON TO TELL YOU how she prays is to invite a demonstration. It's no act, either. For this unpretentious Jamaican woman, prayer and conversation mix easily and naturally. Having addressed you in one sentence, she may address God in the next.

Floretta's conversational style tends to be meek, even tentative. Her prayer, however, is strong and confident. It reveals trust in a God of power who can break into human affairs, who comes to the aid of his people in all sorts of ways.

The following prayer, from a conversation with Floretta, asks for divine intervention in a number of areas. One particular concern for her, perhaps because she lives in a troubled section of Kingston, is the increase of gang warfare and drug-related violence in Jamaica. But Floretta views such situations as raw material for prayer and opportunities for God to demonstrate his power. "What a privilege to carry everything to God in prayer!" she says, quoting from a well-known hymn that seems to express her thoughts exactly.

Almighty God and eternal Father, it's time for you and me to have a little talk again. When I see how things are going in the world, I just have to come and pray for each and every one.

You know, Lord, the times are just upside-down, the entire world seems upside-down at times. Things aren't setting right.

But this world is in your keep, Lord Jesus,
and so I am looking to you and counting on you.
This whole world is at stake, Lord,
and so I am asking you to ride in
   with your quickening power.
Take control, Lord Jesus!

Jesus, you know the hearts of people today.
Search them. Go into their lives. Let them and you come
   together, Lord, so they can be part of your people.
Guide and shelter them, dearest Father.
And if there's something in their lives that's not looking
   right, I'm asking you to help them turn over their leaf.

Remember the people behind prison walls. Give them
   help and strength, dearest Jesus.
Remember the gunman and the ice-pick man [ice picks
   are sometimes used as weapons in Jamaica].
Many evil things they intend to do, my God, and you see
   them all. Stop them and take control. But be merciful
   to them and gather them underneath your wing.

Remember all the children, Lord,
   and shelter them from danger.
And remember *my* children.
Sometimes they are so disobedient.
But you know everything about them, and I'm asking you
   to watch over them.

Remember all the people in government, O Lord, and
   help them.
Remember the leaders of all the different churches.
Help all of them to do what is right.

Floretta Thompson's serene smile comes from her trust in God, not from an easy life. Mother of nine children (of whom only three are still living), Floretta was deserted by her husband long ago. She supports herself by buying peas and coconuts at a large market and reselling them at a small profit.

Dearest Jesus, I know not how to pray for all these people
or what to tell you about them.
I only know that I am here before you and that I am
bringing them to you, not knowing where to start or
where to end.
But you know everything, Lord.

And Lord, remember me.
Dearest Father, you know, sometimes I stretch out my
hands to pick a rose, and prickles and thorns block my
way.
But I will never give up, because I know that I am one of
your dearest, although at times I'm so weak.
So I'm asking you to strengthen me.
Give me more faith, wisdom, knowledge, understanding.

I give you thanks, Lord.
I thank you for keeping tender mercy.
Many things I don't know, but I know that it is you who
put breath in me. It is you who put life in me.
It is right to praise you and give you thanks and trust
you.
Even when the world looks so upside down.
And so I don't give up hopes. I count on you, Jesus, and I
will continue praying—in the morning, in the midday,
all the day long, standing, sitting, or walking.

So take control, dearest Lord,
because none of us is in the keep of ourself.
The world is in the keep of you.
Dearest Jesus, ride in with your quickening power!

*God has provided everything from wedding cakes
to healing of drug addiction.*

The Master Will Supply

On June 17, 1996, Federico Craig and his wife, Dorrit, marked their twenty-fifth anniversary—not of their wedding day (which came a bit later) but of the day each one accepted God's call to service in the Salvation Army. And twenty-five years of service it has been, with stints in Panama (his native country), Belize, Costa Rica, Nicaragua, Trinidad, Barbados, and for the last eight years, Jamaica (her native country).

This latest assignment finds the couple living with their family at the Salvation Army center in Kingston's inner city. Major Craig (the title reflects his many years in the church) directs this "multi-purpose center," which includes a men's hostel, soup kitchen and mobile feeding program, missing persons bureau, drug rehabilitation center, and other outreaches. "It's not an easy job," he comments good-naturedly. "I do it because my life is in the Master's hand, and I believe he has called me into this service."

Major Craig's relaxed, jovial manner makes it clear that he does not view this as a grim sentence. On the contrary. As he explains here, those who seek to answer God's call can count on his loving intervention to provide everything they need for a joyful, fruitful life.

Major Craig, what is your approach to praying for your daily material needs?
First of all, I believe that if I am doing what God has called me to do, as faithfully as I can, then God will provide the rest. Of course, I must be doing this work in response to God and not because I want praise from the people around me. And I must know the dif-

Early morning finds Federico Craig settling down in the family kitchen for a time of personal prayer and Bible reading—a critical point of contact with the Master who called him into his service. Major Craig was eighteen when he gave his life to the Lord at a Salvation Army meeting. The theme that Sunday was taken from Isaiah 6:8, in which the Lord asks, "Whom shall I send?" and the prophet responds, "Here am I! Send me." Major Craig responded too, and he's been "sent" ever since.

ference between wants and needs. For example, right now I might say I want a house. But do I really need one? No, because my family and I live at the Salvation Army center. Or I might say I want a car. I don't need that either, though, because I drive a Salvation Army car. It's just that sometimes I might want to point to something like a house or a car and say, "This is *mine*." But I can't count on God to provide such things, because they're not really needs.

When it comes to the real necessities of life, however, God is able and faithful. He supplies all—and I underline all—my needs! I believe firmly that as God's servant, as his child, everything he has is mine. It is all there for me if I call out in faith, believing that he will provide. And so when I have a particular material need, I pray about it once and then leave it to God. I do not repeatedly ask him, "When? Where? How are you going to meet this need?" I try to leave it to God the way my Master did when he said, "Not my will but thine be done."

Can you recall any specific examples from your own life where God answered your prayer for some material need?
God provides for us every day! But there are moments that stand out.

You know, in the Salvation Army we receive a fixed salary. But since we are more like volunteer workers than employees, this is not a very large sum—more like an allowance to help us along the way. Dorrit and I were both in the Salvation Army in Panama when we decided to get married, and so neither of us had money for the wedding. We presented our need to God and waited. Three weeks before the big day, the person who was in charge of the Salvation Army in our area called to ask if everything was ready for the wedding. "No, not everything," I said. He took it from there and others stepped in as well—and to make a long story short, our entire wedding was prepared without our having to spend a cent. It was a beautiful wedding too!

Something similar happened about a month before the first of our three sons was born. "Where are we going to get the money for the diapers?" my wife wanted to know. "I'm not worried," I told her. "I know the Lord is going to provide all that." I prayed. And once again I got a call from a Salvation Army leader: "Listen, we're going to have a baby shower for your wife. It's a surprise, so don't tell her. But we wanted you to know so that you wouldn't go out and waste your money." God's answer to prayer once again!

Do you see God intervene to meet other kinds of needs as well?
Yes, I see dramatic answers to prayer, many of them in my work with the substance abusers in our rehabilitation center. These are guys who are addicted to cocaine, marijuana, heroin, alcohol—you name it. Some grew up in families where there was no father to give them the training they needed. Some turned to drug dealing for economic reasons. All have been in prison because of their involvement with drugs. Well, God has really turned some of these guys around. They have asked him for help, and he has provided what they needed to get clean and stay clean.

One young man I worked with last year—a very nice, very intelligent fellow in his early twenties—is a customs broker who got involved with drugs when he went to work in the States. He was sent back to Jamaica, but his problem increased, and soon he was in and out of jail because of it. "Can you do something for this man?" someone asked me. "If the court is willing to release him to me, then I will accept him into our program," I said. The court agreed, and so this man was brought to us in handcuffs, bruised and beaten from a fight with drug dealers.

He spent four months at our center. During that time, he received counseling and also began to attend church services. One day it finally became clear to him that God was the only one who could deliver him from his addiction. He confessed his sins, admitted his weakness, and called out to God in faith. As a result, that man is living a normal life today. He's clean and he's back at work. And, yes, he goes to church.

When you pray informally in the course of the day, how do you talk to God about your needs?

I don't usually talk to him only about needs, and my prayer is sometimes very short. It might be a simple request for patience in dealing with someone, or for protection and guidance as I go out. Or if someone says, "Major, please remember me in your prayers," I might stop right there and pray with them for their need. I am not ashamed to pray with anybody, anywhere!... In fact, why don't we pray right now?

O God, our Father, we thank you for this, another day.
We thank you because you love us in spite of our weakness and failures. You care for us. You provide for us.

And so we come to you now, praying that you will forgive us and that you will help us go forth to serve you in the remaining portion of this day, with the Holy Spirit guiding and directing.
Thank you for the work that you have called us to do.
Help us to do it sincerely, for your sake and your approval—not as wanting to please man but wanting to please you.
Help us to serve you humbly, not taking the credit for what you enable us to do—for on our own, we can do nothing.
Open our understanding so that we will do all those things that you would like us to do for the people around us,
things that will really benefit them.
Make us able to see their needs and find a solution to them.

Help us to trust in you always for our every need,
knowing that we are your beloved children and that you
hold us safely in your hand.
May we see many answers to our prayers and watch you at
work in our own lives and in the lives of other people.

And may we stay in constant contact with you, Lord.
Because if we lose contact with you we lose everything.

We praise and glorify you and magnify your name, O God
our Father. Accept again our thanks for this day, for we
offer this prayer in the name of Jesus Christ. Amen.

"God, you see what I need. And you are
bigger than my problem."

I Shall Not Want

"I HAVE MANY, MANY MIRACLES IN MY LIFE!" Of this, Marie
Céres Marcelus is quite convinced. It must be this certainty of
God's action on her behalf that accounts for the joy which
illumines Marie's face, for her life does not seem to hold much
other cause for rejoicing.

Marie lives in a poor section of Port-au-Prince, Haiti, with
her husband and four children, ages twelve, eight, three, and
nine months. Neither she nor her husband can find work,
which means that every day is a struggle for life. Food, clothing,
shelter, medicine, even water—none of these basics is a given for
this woman and her family. And yet, because Marie has seen
God intervene and provide time and time again, her prayer is
trusting, anxiety-free, and not fixated on material needs. In fact,
Marie's first prayer is always for spiritual nourishment:

"I know that man does not live by bread alone but by the
words of God," she explains, "and so I always ask God for
spiritual food first. I ask for more faith so that I can be spiritually full. After he gives me the spiritual bread, the material
bread will come. God is my master, and so I tell him, 'Take
my life and direct me. Because if you teach me, I will learn; if I
teach myself, I won't ever know any better.' I know that without God's word of teaching and direction, life would be very
tough for me."

This may well be the most impressive miracle in Marie's
life—the fact that, in her poverty, she seeks first the kingdom
of God and teaches her children to do the same. But here are
some of the "miracle stories" that Marie will tell you when
you ask what God has done for her.

Marie Céres Marcelus loves to pray—alone or with others, especially in home prayer groups. In the middle of a conversation, she breaks into a spontaneous recitation of Psalm 23, expressing her confidence in the Good Shepherd's care and power.

Very often when I ask God for something, I get it by faith. For example, I wasn't married when I began to have children, I was living in sin. This really bothered me because I wanted to follow God and do his work, but I couldn't see a way out of my problem. So I prayed very hard that God would arrange for me to get married and correct my situation—and he did!

God has healed me often, too. Twice when I was pregnant, the doctor told me that I would need to have the baby by Caesarean. But I had no money and no time for that. Again I prayed and I told the Lord, "I know you are more powerful than the doctor. Sure, he can operate on me to deliver this baby safely, but you can operate on me too so that I don't need this surgery." And those two births were normal.

Another time, I was very sick. I had acid in my stomach and although I had managed to get some medicine, I wasn't getting any better. So one day I put my hand on my stomach and I prayed: "God, your hand is my hand, and my hand is your hand. Please heal me." Right away, he did. I never had that pain again.

Food is another thing I pray for often, and God provides it in many ways. So often I have nothing at all to give my children, and I say to God, "You are bigger than my problem, and you see my need even before I ask." And just as I'm thinking we will have nothing to eat that day, suddenly someone comes along with money or food—a relative or a brother or sister in the Lord. And I know that this gift is not coming just from a human person: it is God who sends it to me, God who directed this person to help.

God loves me a lot. He loves me a lot. He takes care of me and my family every day. That's why I can say I have many, many miracles in my life.

The Lord is my shepherd, I shall not want.
He makes me lie down in green pastures;
he leads me beside still waters;
he restores my soul.
He leads me in right paths
for his name's sake.

Even though I walk through the darkest valley,
I fear no evil;
for you are with me;
your rod and your staff—
they comfort me.

You prepare a table before me
in the presence of my enemies;
you anoint my head with oil;
my cup overflows.
Surely goodness and mercy shall follow me
all the days of my life,
and I shall dwell in the house of the Lord
my whole life long.   Psalm 23

"Prayer and faith won't work for this,"
the doctor said.

But God Makes the
Impossible Possible

HIS WEEKLY TV BROADCAST reaches thousands of homes in Jamaica. Faith Cathedral Deliverance Centre, the independent Pentecostal church he began in 1978, is the largest congregation in the country, with a membership of some three thousand adults and fifteen hundred children. Inspired by his example, spin-off churches have arisen: eighteen in Jamaica, five in the U.S., two in Canada, one in the Cayman Islands. Under his leadership the church has developed a school, a factory, a dental clinic, a soup kitchen, and self-help projects that provide funds and advice for launching small businesses.

Small wonder that Bishop Herro Blair is a well-known figure in every corner of Jamaica!

Nothing in this forty-nine-year-old preacher's early life portended such extensive recognition, however. As Bishop Blair likes to put it, "I was born in poverty and raised in obscurity," the seventh child in a family of fourteen children. Home was a two-bedroom, thatched, wattle-and-daub house in a little village eleven miles out of Montego Bay, on Jamaica's north coast. Not until he was nine did Bishop Blair ever leave that village—or put a pair of shoes on his feet.

Bishop Blair's father was a traveling preacher who often walked twenty miles to preach in rural congregations too poor to repay him with anything but the most meager offerings. "Sometimes he received a couple of pounds of yams, some bananas, a few breadfruit," Bishop Blair remembers. "On many occasions he would come back home without a dime and tell my mother, 'Sorry, honey. I didn't get an offering this week.'"

Growing up in a poor preacher's family, Herro Blair "hated preaching and wouldn't touch it with a long stick"—not until he was filled with the Holy Spirit on his nineteenth birthday. Now he preaches to thousands every Sunday, in this church where "we simply pray, and God works miracles."

Bishop Blair's memories of those early hardships leave him with no desire to return to a life of poverty. "If having faith in God means you always have to subsist on mangoes and yam seeds, sleep on a dirt floor and watch the moon peeping through the cane leaf shingles, share a school uniform with your brother and be able to go to class only every other week—who wants that?" He rejects the view that Christians must be poor and preaches instead that God intends people to prosper.

On the other hand, Bishop Blair is grateful for the training that came out of his childhood experiences. "I thank God for where I was born, for the conditions I was born in," he insists. "For those conditions have conditioned my life and shown me where always to look for my help. *My help comes from the Lord, who made heaven and earth.*"

Most of all, he is grateful for the example of his parents who—now in their eighties—still stimulate him to prayer and to a deeper life of faith. One faith-building incident that marked Bishop Blair took place before he was born.

When my mother was pregnant with me, six doctors tried to convince her to have an abortion. "You're too poor to have another child," they told her. "You won't survive; your health isn't good enough. And don't you know there are too many people in Jamaica already?" But my father objected. "Doctor, there is a soul at stake here, and it belongs to God. And what if this baby were to become a preacher some day? I would never want to think that I had destroyed a preacher's life."

And so, because of my parents' faith and reverence for life, I came into this world.

Typical of his mother's strong faith, says Bishop Blair, was how she reacted when it was mealtime and the family had nothing to eat.

She never fussed or quarreled with my father when he didn't have anything to give for the family's survival. She just prayed and believed that some way or another, God would provide, one day at a time. I would see her put the cooking pot on the fire and bring the water to a boil, singing all the while, without having any idea where the food to put into that pot was going to come from. But before the water had boiled down, somebody would rap on the gate—a girl or a boy with a basket of food or something like that—and we would eat for another day.

Such incidents made a lasting impression not just on him but on all his brothers and sisters, says Bishop Blair.

All of us are the benefactors of our parents' prayer life. So now whenever we come into a hard place, wherever we find mountains blocking our way and places where no doors are made, we understand that the impossible can be made possible through faith and prayer. We have seen those things happen before! So it's very easy now to believe God for anything. Absolutely anything.

In Bishop Blair's case, this early training is reflected in two characteristics of his Faith Cathedral congregation. "It's a praying congregation," where an hour of prayer precedes every church service and where prayer teams in a special "Upper Room" intercede around the clock for special needs. And it's a congregation where miracles take place, says Bishop Blair.

I would say that if our ministry at Faith Cathedral becomes well known, it will be as a result of the miracles that God performs here through prayer. There are so many cases of healings and answered prayers, and some of them are incredible.

A man who had been crippled for over seven years was

brought to our service one Sunday morning. He was unable to walk, so he was put in a wheelchair and brought down the aisle for prayer. All we did was pray a psalm and sing a chorus, "There Is Power in the Blood." And he got up and was able to walk!

Miracles like this are a powerful stimulant to faith—and especially so when they happen to you.

One Saturday evening four or five years ago I was getting the church ready for my television broadcast the next morning. A few young men were helping me to put up a drape for the backdrop. I was up on a ladder about twenty-five feet from the floor when somebody called the young man who was steadying my ladder. He let go and before I could bat an eye, I was on the ground, lying flat on my back at the edge of the baptismal pool. I lay there for about twenty-five minutes till the paramedics came, feeling like parts of my body had been scattered all over the place.

When I was rushed to the hospital, x-rays showed that my body was intact but that my number one lumbar vertebra was broken. The vertebra had been severed, leaving a half-inch gap between the ends of the bone. The doctor looked at me and said, "Well, I know you're a man of faith, but prayer and faith can't work for this. Practicality has to work." He told me I would have to be in traction for eight weeks—no getting up, no moving at all.

"Doctor," I answered, "I am a man of faith. But I have never in my life been sick and so I have never had to prove God for anything physical. Please send me home, because I would like to see what God can do about this."

"That's impossible. You cannot leave the hospital."

We negotiated, and finally he agreed that I could leave at my own risk but that I absolutely must remain immobile for two months. So I was back home that Saturday evening, and my wife tended to me and people from the church came and prayed with me. The next morning I remained in bed. It was the first Sunday that I was missing services in this church, and I didn't like it.

The following Sunday I said to my wife, "I want to go to church." It was seven weeks earlier than what the doctor had ordered, but to church I was taken. That day the preacher preached on having the faith of God. It was just the right word for me! I prayed a little prayer asking God to heal me and then I stepped up out of my chair, went before the people, and asked them to stretch out their hands and pray for me. Then I prayed for those who were sick.

After the service I slipped away into my office. Never before had I been in such pain! It was as if the devil were saying to me, "See? The doctor was right after all. Faith and prayer don't work for this." I lay down on the floor for fifteen minutes and then had to be taken back home.

But I didn't stop believing God for my healing and, as it turned out, that episode in my office was just a test of faith. The following week, I was back in church preaching. And I was never troubled by that problem again.

I did go back to the doctor, though, to get my healing documented. The nurse brought in my file; the doctor looked through it and then he threw it into the garbage. "It's not possible," he said. "I'm not going to be a fool. You can go your way." I finally persuaded him to examine me and to do an x-ray. "That can't be the same bone," he said when he got the results and compared them against the original x-ray. "In this x-ray I measured a half-inch-wide break in the number one lumbar. In this one there's nothing to show that the bone was ever even cracked. There must be some mistake."

But I knew there was no mistake. Through faith and prayer, the impossible can indeed be made possible.

A troubled woman, a sinister presence…

A Prayer That Brought Freedom

YOU MAY HAVE HEARD IT SAID that Haiti is 90 percent Catholic and 100 percent voodoo. This is an unjust characterization that overlooks the presence and faith of the country's many devout Catholics. The grain of truth in this stereotype, however, is that voodoo does exercise a hold over some Haitians. And, with its strange blend of Catholic devotions and pagan African religions, it exposes people to spiritual dangers.

"Evil spirits really do exist," says Haitian-born Father Joseph Simon, "and when people choose to dabble in the occult, in things like voodoo, they open themselves up to diabolical manifestations." Father Simon shares the story below not so much to illustrate the reality of this malevolent spiritual world as to testify to Jesus' triumph over all powers of darkness.

One day a mother and father came to see me to tell me that their eighteen-year-old daughter had an evil spirit. I was surprised by this, since I was acquainted with the family and knew that they attended the Catholic church nearby. But they had moved here from the country, where voodoo practices are more prevalent and people are more easily drawn to the occult in their search for a better life. The devil can take advantage of such inclinations and, from what this couple said, he did indeed seem to have gained some foothold in the family.

The parents were becoming increasingly alarmed by the strange things that were going on with their daughter. She would shriek during the night, they told me. She would thrash and struggle, and her strength was extraordinary: five people couldn't hold her down. Also, she wanted nothing to do with prayer—although in the past she had enjoyed praying in church and at prayer meetings.

His car is a rattletrap, his resources limited, but Salesian Father Joseph Simon seems to have inherited some of the cheerful faith of St. John Bosco. (That's his statue behind Father Simon.) "The great grace we have received is that we are never discouraged but always have a zest for our work!" the priest explains. "Prayer is behind all this, and I do pray constantly, everywhere, expressing myself very simply to my Father."

So I went to the family's home, and it really did seem that an evil spirit was at work in this young woman. Sometimes when she spoke, her voice was different and you sensed that another person was speaking through her. In this strange voice, the evil spirit had threatened to prevent her from going to church or to prayer meetings. Apparently the threat had been carried out, because, by the time I saw the girl, one of her legs had become so swollen that she could no longer walk. This condition had no apparent cause, either. I took the girl to the doctor myself, and x-rays revealed no physical problem whatsoever.

So her parents and I prayed with the young woman, and this evil spirit speaking through her said that if we continued, he would make her blind. We continued—and then one day she could no longer see.

Convinced that something demonic was going on, I asked for the prayer support of a local nun through whom the Lord has worked many miracles. One evening we went to meet this nun—the young woman and I, along with the five people needed to carry the invalid into my car and up and down stairs.

Sister and I had just a short time of prayer with the girl, but it was intense and full of faith. First we prayed a decade of the rosary. Then, very simply, we asked for God's help.

Lord Jesus, we ask you to come to our aid and deliver this young woman from the power of the devil.
You are capable of doing this for her.
We believe in you.
And so we ask you with faith, Lord, to let this young woman suffer no longer but to free her from this affliction.
Thank you, Lord.
Come, Lord Jesus!

When we had finished praying, I made a cross on the girl's eyes and Sister said, "Now, in the name of Jesus, begone, you evil spirit, and let this girl see again." She opened her eyes and was able to see clearly—as she immediately proved when we gave her a Bible to read aloud from.

Then Sister told her, "You were carried in here, but you're going to be able to walk out on your own. The devil will leave you in peace now." And the swollen leg returned to its normal size! The young woman walked out free, rejoicing in God's goodness and power. She has been untroubled ever since.

This demonstration of God's power, in which I was an eyewitness and a participant, has spurred me to greater faith and confidence as I go about my ordinary work. No matter what obstacles I may encounter, God is there to help me as I turn to him in prayer—and he has already triumphed over every obstacle!

The "ordinary work" that Father Simon mentions above is with students and also with street kids in Pétionville, a suburb of Port-au-Prince. "I try to evangelize the two extremes," he explains: "those young people who are studying philosophy and reflecting on the meaning of life, and also those who live on the street and feel beaten down by life every day."

Father Simon's initiatives on behalf of homeless children are his response to the mandate given by the nineteenth-century founder of the religious order he belongs to: "St. John Bosco told us always to go and seek out the very poorest children."

Father Simon began by going out into the streets every Saturday. He would gather a small group of boys and girls, feed them, tend to their wounds and illnesses, have them sing and play, and talk to them about God's love. "What I have always tried to do," he says, "is give them confidence—in God's love for them, in his desire to see them live better lives, in his readiness to help them learn and improve themselves."

For the past three years Father Simon's special project has been to develop a drop-in center that can be a refuge for his little flock when they are sick, beaten, chased, tired, hungry, or just want an encouraging word. "We have a house now," he reports. "Soon we'll be able to provide shelter for some of the poorest children. We'll see what else develops, with God's help!"

CHAPTER SIX

Your Way, Lord, Not Mine

"Believe me," wrote St. Teresa of Avila in one of her classic guides to prayer, "the safest thing is to will only what God wills, for God knows us better than we know ourselves, and loves us."

As the men and women in this chapter have learned, God's will is indeed the best and most secure resting place—but it is not necessarily the most comfortable. Jesus submitted perfectly to his Father's will, yet the description of his agonized prayer in the garden of Gethsemane hardly conveys an impression of painless resignation.

Jesus *did* embrace the Father's plan, however, and he teaches his followers to do the same. He invites us to imitate his trust and absolute surrender and to pray along with him, "My Father, if it is possible, let this cup pass from me: yet not what I want but what you want" (Matthew 26:39).

Self-abandonment to the will of God is the theme that runs through the stories in this chapter. They tell of faith during those times when God did not intervene in desired ways—of urgent prayers that seemed to go unanswered, or had answers that were delayed or that took unexpected forms.

Some of these stories may make us fearful. *Is God going to ask me to do something I don't want to do?* we might worry.

How will I be able to endure it? But the truth is that any life, whether surrendered to God or not, inescapably meets with challenges and dreaded developments, and eventually with death. The men and women in this chapter do not explore the issue of *why* they suffer trials or disappointments. But their stories show *how* such challenges can be met: by trusting in God's grace and in his loving plan for them. In this spirit, self-surrender becomes an act of love.

*"For years I didn't talk to God. I was
too afraid of what he might say."*

Running Scared

HE IS WHAT YOU CALL A "LATE VOCATION," this hulk of a man
with the build of a football player. Father Burchell McPherson
was ordained a priest of the Catholic Church five years ago at
age forty. He still can't quite figure out exactly what it was
that drew him into the Church as an adult convert. But he is
perfectly clear about what brought him into the priesthood.

> After I became a Catholic, I started attending a church in a very
> poor neighborhood west of Kingston. It was during this time
> that I woke up to the needs of the poor. I began working with
> them—teaching Sunday school, visiting the sick, and serving as I
> could.
>
> Sometimes people would say to me, "Have you thought
> about the priesthood?" I had not. Becoming a priest was just
> not on my agenda. Whether or not it was in God's plans for me,
> I wasn't sure; I only knew that it wasn't in mine. I used to come
> to the Lord and present him with my hopes: "Lord, this is what I
> want to achieve in life." I certainly didn't want to ask any ques-
> tions about what *he* might want.
>
> For that reason there were years when I never really prayed.
> Oh, I pretended to—both to myself and to others. But I was just
> running through prayers in a book and then disappearing as fast
> as I could. I wasn't talking honestly with God, and I certainly
> wasn't listening. I was too afraid of what he might say! What if
> he did want me to be a priest after all?
>
> When I was in my late twenties, though, I started to tire of
> running. *I wonder what God wants me to do with my life?* I asked
> myself. Finally I got up the courage to go away to a retreat cen-

In Father Burchell McPherson's eyes you can read concern for the children—for their education, their future, and especially their family life. The absence of fathers is a big problem in his neighborhood, says Father McPherson, who serves the people of St. Pius X parish in Kingston, Jamaica.

ter, a place where I could stay for a while to seek the Lord and get advice. It took me about a month to reach the decision that I wanted to become a deacon. As a deacon I could preach, preside at weddings and baptisms, and do other things to assist a priest—but without having to be ordained to the priesthood. *And that will be enough,* I decided. *Full stop. Beyond this I don't want to go.*

But I still hadn't really consulted the Lord. You know, sometimes we go to the Lord and think we are talking to him but we are really talking to ourselves!

Time passed. I proceeded with my new plan and got involved with many kinds of church work. And then one evening—I'm still not quite sure how it happened—I found myself praying about the very issues I had avoided for years. Somehow it struck me that it was really the Lord I was addressing. Very simply, very honestly, I took the step of talking to him about my life and the priesthood. I was able to let go of my fears and plans enough to tell him, "If this is your will, let it be done." I was even able to listen to what he had to say!

That type of honest communication with the Lord was very important in the years that followed. Even after I went into the seminary, there were days when I felt like giving it all up and pursuing my old plans. "Why?" I would ask the Lord. "Why am I here in this situation? Priesthood is not for me." But always when I talked to him, the Lord would encourage me and renew my desire to serve his people as a priest.

Even today I find it very important to tell the Lord how I feel. And I still ask him, "Why am I in this situation?"—especially when it's six o'clock in the morning and people are banging on my door because they want something!

The community I serve is a very poor one, with few resources and many needs. I get frustrated and impatient sometimes. I feel pushed to the edge, like I want to give up on people. What helps me is to sit down in the presence of the Lord and talk to him honestly about whatever is going on. I question him, too—not always in a good way, but at least I am communicating! Then I keep quiet and listen to him. And this whole process strengthens my faith.

One thing I realize again and again through prayer is that when Jesus invited me to follow him, he did not say, "Come, Burchell, things are going to be easy." No, he offered me a life of denying myself and taking up my cross. So of course there will be trials, persecution, suffering, ups and downs. But these things are unavoidable, and it doesn't make sense to run from them. Now I just run with them to the Lord!

Am I glad I took a look at God's agenda for my life and became a priest? Overall, yes. I feel that I'm where God wants me, and I'm very comfortable working in this community, even though many people might not want to identify with it.

I like to walk around, talk to people, see how they live. I think it's important for a priest to be seen not just on Sunday morning in church but out in the neighborhood during the week. So I go down to the corner and rap with the men playing dominoes. I visit homes, keep in touch with the children at our parish school, stop and talk to the women doing laundry. And I see God working in these people, even at times when they are struggling. When I listen to their testimonies of how God is with them and helps them through hard times—that gives me strength.

Another thing that encourages me and makes me feel I'm in the right place is that people are supporting me and working with me to build this church community. That's a big change.

When I came to this parish after ordination, I found security guards here. Vandalism and theft were big problems. You couldn't leave your car outside overnight. Every Monday we had to replace the toilet bowls in the school bathrooms: people would break them and take them out and sell them. Even the church was getting broken into. "You should get guard dogs," I was told. But that didn't make sense to me. Building a church and having guards and guns and dogs—to my mind, those things just don't go together!

Instead I got rid of the guards and began working to build a sense of community. "This isn't *my* church and *my* school," I would tell the people. "It belongs to all of *you*. I'm here to work along with you, not to run everything." Gradually, they got the idea. Now we have leaders popping up. Maybe they can't read or write, some of them, but they have leadership qualities and they can do a lot. "The Lord isn't just interested in people with college degrees," I assure the people. "He's calling each one of you. He has a plan for what you can contribute. And it's a good plan."

After all those years of fighting God's plan for my own life and then discovering how good it really was, I should know!

It's always easier to say, "Your way, Lord, not mine," when you see God intervene to answer prayer. Father Burchell cites the following "faith story" as just one incident that has encouraged him to persevere in his vocation of service and prayer.

The Day the Rice Ran Out

Because of all the material needs in this community, the parish has a lot of social outreach programs. We teach skills, provide medical and dental care, try to help people get out of shacks and into decent housing. We also distribute free food every Friday. It's not much—about four pounds of rice or flour or cornmeal or whatever we can get—but it's very important to the 150 or so people who line up for it each week.

One week during a time when rice was scarce, I realized that the way it was looking, there would be no food to give out that Friday. You couldn't buy rice in the shops, and no one had any rice to give us—not even Food For The Poor. I called their office on Thursday morning and was told, "Sorry, we have no rice available."

That day the lady who oversees our food distribution told me, "Father, we have no food to give out tomorrow. What do we do?" I reassured her. "When the people come, we'll have Mass and pray with them as usual. The Lord will provide somewhere along the line."

I believed what I had said, but in private that Friday morning, I repeated our concern to the Lord and told him exactly how I felt.

God, there is no food. What do we do? You know how much these people depend on this rice. Some of them are really, really in need. What's going to happen to them? Now I don't know what you have in mind, but I'm going to feel really bad if they have to go back to their kids with nothing.

And Lord, if I send these people home hungry, the guilt is not only on my shoulders; it's on your shoulders too, because you promised to look after your children.

But I know you are with us and will do something.

And that's what I told the people at Mass that morning. I explained the situation and then I gave a sermon on how Jesus fed the crowds with only five barley loaves and two fish. "Those people were hungry, too, and look at what Jesus did for them," I pointed out. "I don't know exactly what the Lord is going to do for us here today, but it's the same Jesus, and he still cares about hungry people. I know something will happen."

Something did happen, too. While I was still celebrating Mass, I saw the Food For The Poor truck drive up through the gates. And from the altar, I could see what was being unloaded: bags of rice—enough for everyone. I stood there, not believing my eyes, remembering how I'd been told, "Sorry, no rice." But as I learned later, a shipment had suddenly arrived....

And so once again, I was reminded of the Lord's constant care and presence. He provides and he multiplies—food, time, patience, and whatever else is needed, at the moment it's needed. And that's the reason I'm still here!

Mother of six, grandmother of nineteen, great-grand-mother of twenty, Evelyn Mahfood never thought her active life would be ended by a robber's bullet. Prayer has helped her make the transition to paralysis with forgiveness, not anger, in her heart. "I've been close to God all my life," she says with a gentle smile. "But if I tell you that I pray more now, I won't be lying."

The gunman backed up and pointed his gun at me...

Please, God, Forgive Them
By Evelyn Mahfood

OCTOBER 5, 1992. I glanced out past the doors of the veranda to find my usually magnificent view of Kingston harbor hidden behind heavy sheets of rain. The storm that had been threatening all day had finally broken with a vengeance, dissipating the thick and sultry air with terrific bursts of wind and crashes of thunder. *I wish this would let up a bit.* I didn't relish the thought of going out into this torrential downpour. But then, I had been through many turbulent rainy seasons since coming to Jamaica as a young bride in 1936. How strange everything had seemed at first—the climate, the food, the way of life so different from what I had grown up with in Beirut, Lebanon. How homesick I had been!

But I had adjusted, and our years in Jamaica had been good ones for my husband and me. His business had prospered. Six healthy children had been born to us. I glanced lovingly at their photos on the piano. They were long grown up by now and some of them lived far away: Mary Louise had moved to Detroit, Ferdinand and Robin to Florida, Pamela to Beirut; only Sam and Joe had remained in Jamaica.

I was so proud of all our children. We had always tried to raise them in the love of God, and now they were trying to raise their own beautiful children the same way. I was especially proud of how well our four boys worked together in the family business they had taken over after my husband's death. Even now, with Ferdy working full-time for the poor, they helped one another out.

I had been pleased and happy as Ferdy's commitment to the poor developed. "This is a beautiful vocation," I told my son. "Keep it up."

Of course, I didn't know then how deeply Ferdy's decision would affect my life. But he had introduced me to a Jamaica that was far removed from my privileged world. Through him I had met so many desperately needy people who were being crushed by hunger and poverty and disease. Ferdy had helped me to reach out and help them.

I thought back to a school he had put me in touch with. When I visited, I was shocked to discover how hungry the children were. "You come to me," I told the director. "I'm going to give you food and a kitchen and a refrigerator and pots and pans. And you feed those children. They look hungry!"

Now, at eighty, I was continuing my efforts. My already busy life had become fuller than ever with visits to the schools and centers I was helping out. My garage was packed with bags of rice and kidney beans, which I distributed to the poor. My home was open to the groups of journalists and Food For The Poor workers who often accompanied Ferdy to Jamaica; I loved to share with them what I had discovered about the joy of helping the needy. I loved to feed them, too, though it took days to prepare the traditional Lebanese dishes I always served. But I never minded the work—not even when it meant hosting 36 dinner guests, as I had done only four days before.

The sound of pelting rain roused me from my thoughts. I took a look at the time. Almost four o'clock. *Better hurry if I want to make this meeting.* I didn't want to keep Father Ramkissoon and the bishop waiting. I had already helped Father with a little nursery for handicapped children. Today was the blessing and official opening of his latest project. "The Evelyn Mahfood Home for Unwed Mothers," he had insisted on calling it. "All right, Father," I had agreed with a laugh. "Whatever you say!"

Purse in hand, I walked through the dining room and out into the carport, pulling the grille-work door shut behind me. I'd have called out a goodbye to the servants, but today the house was empty. They had all retreated to their own separate quarters, and my driver, Oakley, had gone to the farm where my son Sam grows bird of paradise flowers. Sam and Joe didn't like it when I went out by myself, but I felt perfectly capable of driving around Kingston, even when it meant going into the more dangerous sections. And when Oakley was with me, I often drove him!

I eased the car out into the rain and moved slowly towards the long driveway with its hairpin turns. Suddenly, out of nowhere, two young men dressed completely in black appeared and blocked my way menacingly. One held the kind of big knife that I call a cutlass; it's a sort of machete that field workers use to open coconuts and cut sugar cane. The other held a gun with a silencer.

Robbers, I thought. *They must be poor and hungry.* I was startled but not afraid, not even when the one with the machete smashed my window and snatched the keys out of the ignition.

"What do you want?" I asked him calmly.

"Whatever you have." He grabbed at the chain around my neck.

"Here is my purse." I reached for my bag and was turning to hand it over when I saw the gunman back up two paces and raise his gun. He aimed and shot.

The bullet hit me in the neck. My hands slipped off the steering wheel, my foot off the accelerator. Blood began streaming from the wound, flowing down over my dress and onto the seat. I slumped, unable to move but feeling no pain. And I could still talk.

"Man, why did you do that to me? I love you. I do harm to no one. And I love the poor."

My assailant seemed suddenly unnerved. He turned to his friend with a confused look. He stared at his gun as though wishing to undo what he had just done.

"You love me? Why?"

"I love you and I love the poor," I answered him. "You did this because you are hungry. I have plenty food for you in the garage. Go and take some." But they just stood there gaping, with the pouring rain slicking down their hair and matting their clothes.

So I continued. "You didn't have to shoot me," I reproached them. "I would always give. And it is not good for you to steal."

That was about all I could manage to say, but I could see by the men's faces that my words had shaken them. They ran off and though they did help themselves to the beans and rice, they left everything else untouched.

Will I live through this? I wondered. I felt so weak and there was so much blood. *Lord, please take care of me. And send someone to help.*

Oakley was the one who discovered me an hour later. "My missus is dead! My missus is dead!" he began crying out when he spotted me lying on the car floor covered with blood. "Oakley," I interrupted, "please take me to the hospital." I wouldn't resist his driving me this time.

News spread fast and soon my family and friends had gathered by my bedside at the hospital. By this time, I felt terrible pain in my neck and shoulders. *At least I won't need surgery,* I thought gratefully. The bullet had gone right through my neck and although the doctors couldn't promise anything, they were hopeful that in time I would recover completely.

What has happened instead, in the years since that fateful October day, is something that any active person could only dread. After months of hospitalization and agonizing physical therapy, I did indeed come back home—but hardly to the same life.

Now when I take in the beautiful view of Kingston from my veranda, I do so from a wheelchair. My hands rest helplessly on little white pillows on my lap. With my second and third vertebrae shattered, I am completely paralyzed from the shoulders down. I must rely on others to take care of me, for I cannot perform even the smallest task. If a mosquito lands on my neck, someone else must swat it for me.

My life is still busy, and I still sponsor a number of projects that serve the poor. But my visits to schools and centers and homes are fewer now; I do more of my work by phone. I can't host those big dinners any more. And every day includes hours of that dreaded physical therapy.

"Please give me patience," I ask the Lord many times a day. These changes have been hard. And so I pray more now—for myself as I learn to live with suffering; for those I love, that they may be spared such an ordeal; for the poor, who experience suffering in so many ways.

And, of course, I always pray for those two young men. Sometimes I even dream about them. *Who are they? Where are they now?* They were never caught, and I can't help but wonder. *Were they changed through our encounter?* This side of heaven, I will probably never know. But how I hope to see them again one day in paradise, perhaps in the company of the good thief that Jesus forgave from the cross!

For that reason, from the moment of the shooting till this very day, I have never stopped praying: "Please, God, forgive them."

He lives at St. Monica's Home for the Abandoned Elderly, in Kingston, Jamaica, but George McPhee feels anything but abandoned. "The Lord is always with me, and I talk to him at all times," he declares. Furthermore, this is a two-way conversation: "The Holy Spirit speaks to me in a still, small voice and gives me encouragement and direction. So although I am visually handicapped, sometimes I see things spiritually."

> *"I love the Lord, and I love the Lord
> to have his way with me."*

God Knows Best

THE NAME GETS RIGHT DOWN TO BUSINESS. St. Monica's Home for the Abandoned Elderly. Twenty-nine men and women live here; a handful of them bear the marks of Hansen's disease (leprosy). One of these is seventy-four-year-old George McPhee, a resident of St. Monica's for almost fifteen years.

It is sweltering in the director's office, where George sits talking, and the oscillating fan is no match for this thick, oppressive heat. Beads of sweat form on George's bald head, drip down onto eyelids half-open over sightless eyes, gather in rivulets to trickle over ravaged features, and finally fall onto George's red tee shirt. Every now and then George mops his head with a little towel.

George is blind and disfigured but so animated and full of life that his afflictions, as well as the heat, recede into the background as he speaks. His faith is riveting, as is his lively way of sprinkling prayer, song, and poetry into his conversation. "From childhood days, I loved the Lord dearly," George says with emotion. "I don't know why the Lord permitted it!" A gleeful chuckle. "But he knows best. He is a good God. Maybe he formed me this way to keep me near to him."

God knows best. This is George's trusting perspective not just on his love of God but on his general lot in life. "If I was enjoying good health and had a lot of material things, maybe I would stray away from the Lord," he muses.

Behind George's simple acceptance, you suspect, lies a long apprenticeship in learning to surrender.

George was in his twenties when he noticed a suspicious spot on his face. He was a simple farmer then, unmarried and living with his sister and her family. "I planted all kinds of little things and had small livestock, chickens and such," he reminisces. "I love the soil very much." The neighbors talked about George's blemish, but he wasn't too concerned at first: "Plenty people thought they had Hansen's disease, and it turned out to be nothing."

But George tested positive. There was no treatment for the disease at the time; victims were simply isolated from the rest of society. So George had to leave farm and family behind and move into a special "Hansen's home." Here he stayed for almost thirty years, until new ways of treating the disease made isolation unnecessary. "You can go," residents of the Hansen's home were told then. "You *must* go," was the real message. The home was being turned into a rehabilitation center for the mentally ill.

But George no longer had a family home to return to. And by this time, although he was free of the disease, he was too handicapped by its effects to be able to take care of himself.

That was a difficult period, George admits. "I was very much concerned about the outcome." Then one night he had a dream.

I was walking through a body of water like the sea, on a sort of beam of iron that was below the surface so that I could not see it. All of a sudden I felt afraid that I might slip. With that, my right foot slipped a little. I stopped, not knowing what to do. Then I heard someone say, "Look up!" As I did, I saw a stout rope come down out of the sky and attach itself firmly under my two arms. I realized then that I need never be afraid. And when I woke up I remembered what the Lord says in his holy word: "When you go through the waters, I will be with you."

In real life, too, there came a last-minute rescue. Through the efforts of Monsignor Richard Albert, a Catholic priest who had learned of the situation, St. Monica's came into being. George and a few other displaced persons from the Hansen's home became its first residents.

Of his personal struggles to come to grips with his illness, George does not say much—only that "the Lord rubbed me down little by little and helped me to accept it." An especially difficult point in the process, he confides, was the loss of his eyesight: "It happened gradually. And I want to tell you, at that time I prayed day and night! I begged the Lord, I reasoned with him, I talked to him—just like two people talk, friend to friend. And yet the blindness happened."

Another critical moment of surrender came during a period of illness, when George was longing for death and union with the Lord in heaven. A dream on two successive nights—about a bright crown of gold that was just out of reach—persuaded him to yield once again to God's plan for him: "I took it that the Lord wanted me to spend some more time down here before he called me home."

Why do bad things happen to good people? This not a subject George agonizes over. His sufferings do not tempt him to call God's love and power into question. "I love the Lord, and I love the Lord to have his way with me," he says simply. "Why should I fret and cry and feel sorry for myself? I just accept it and make the best of it." Based on love, this acceptance is joyful and active. As George sees it, sufferings and hardships are raw material: "You can use every situation for the honor and glory of God! I ask him to make me his good instrument, and I find that although I am so afflicted I can still help others."

"Giving good encouragement" is his main service, says George. This he does through the songs and poems he writes and performs and through his bedside visits to pray with residents who are ill.

What he offers all is a message of truth based on a lifetime of training in self-surrender and loving trust of God. And with everyone he meets, George also offers "a word of prayer."

Loving Father, thank you for your love and mercies. Thank you for your goodness in every way. You are the source of all good things, and we look to you to provide all that we need.

Give us strength and courage to accept our suffering, remembering that Christ was sinless yet he suffered on a cruel cross for the sins of the whole world. Help us, dear Lord, to bear our little cross, to be cheerful and not give up.

You see that we are weak sometimes; we don't really love you as we should. But when we fall, you never get vexed! You are always ready to help us get up and go forward again.

I love you so much, dear Lord, you who have always taken care of me. It is you who send friends to help us here at St. Monica's, and I thank you for each one. You see in my heart that I love them dearly, even though I

don't know them all. Bless them, and if any should happen to read these words, let them be encouraged to love you more and more.

Use us all as your instruments. Help us to love our neighbors as ourselves, and show us what little part you want us to play. Lead us to serve you in Spirit and truth, so that we will run the race to the end and hear you call us home at last.

All these mercies I ask in Jesus' name. Amen.

Drinking from a Saucer

George McPhee spends much of his time writing poems and songs to the glory of God. This poem expresses not only George's cheerful acceptance of difficulties but also his deep gratefulness to the loving God "who knows best."

I have never made a fortune, and it's probably too late now.
I don't worry about that much, I'm happy anyhow.
As I go along life's journey, reaping more than I have sowed,
I'm drinking from a saucer, 'cause my cup has overflowed.

I don't have lots of riches, and sometimes the going is tough.
I have a family that loves me, and that is quite enough.

I thank God for his blessings and his mercies he's
bestowed.
I'm drinking from a saucer, 'cause my cup has overflowed.

I remember times when things went wrong, my faith got
a little thin.
Then all at once the dark clouds broke, and the sun
peeked through again.
Lord, please help me not to gripe about the tough rows
I have hoed.
I'm drinking from a saucer, 'cause my cup has over-
flowed.

If God gives me strength and courage when my way
grows steep and tough,
I'll not ask for other blessings. I'm already blessed
enough.
May I never be too busy to help another bear his load.
I'll keep drinking from a saucer, 'cause my cup has overflowed.

GEORGE MCPHEE

*"Prayer is for asking God,
'What do you want me to do?'"*

God's Timing, Not Mine

AUGUST 26, 1965. Father Jacques Beaudry, a priest of the order of St. Viator, steps onto Haitian soil for the first time. The sea shimmers in the sun's heat. Hibiscus and bougainvillea, palm and avocado and breadfruit trees offer their blooms and fruits. Vendors line the streets peddling sugar cane, mangoes, and other goods unfamiliar to this newcomer from the north. Gaily colored taxis, "tap-taps," with names like *Merci Jésus* and *Surprise* bulge with passengers as they rumble up and down the streets. Women glide through the crowds, balancing astonishingly large loads on their heads: baskets of live chickens, mountains of bright plastic basins, heavy water buckets. Poverty, in the form of beggars and cripples and half-naked children, is extreme and inescapable.

Such sights and sounds and smells—so different from anything this thirty-one-year-old ever experienced back in Quebec, Canada. But amazingly, he immediately feels at home. "Why, it's as if I've always been here," he marvels.

Since boyhood, Jacques Beaudry had wanted to be a missionary. "Why? I don't know. Why does a man choose to marry one woman and not another? I just knew that I deeply desired to give myself in this way."

Jacques was in his teens when this desire came to the surface, in the unlikely setting of a Boy Scout camp where he was a patrol leader. A drama contest was announced one day: each patrol was assigned to prepare a scene from the life of a missionary. "We were to present 'the missionary in a moment of

Father Jacques Beaudry keeps this photo of a sunset in his room as a reminder that "prayer scatters life's darkest clouds and lets us see the sun smiling through." One July evening during a time of political turmoil, Father Beaudry and a group of friends were on the terrace interceding for Haiti. The horizon was "black, black" with clouds as they prayed, "O Lord, if only you would open the heavens and come!" Suddenly "the clouds were torn away, the whole sky opened up, and the sun shone through!" A quick-witted photographer captured the moment.

discouragement.'" As it turned out, Jacques played the missionary and delivered a five-minute monologue so compelling that it won his patrol first place.

> It was a prayer. I remember kneeling on a boulder and crying out to God as I imagined the missionary must have about his disappointments, his suffering over not being able to reach more souls. Strangely, even though this was a performance, something happened to me during that prayer. God used that moment to speak to me about my own vocation.

Five years later, Jacques was about to be ordained as a member of an order that had priests working in Japan and Taiwan. "May I go into the missions?" he had asked the superior upon entering the seminary. "We'll see about that later on," was the reply. Now Jacques repeated his request. The answer was unexpected: "We'd like you to continue studying theology so that you can teach and help prepare others to become priests."

> Obviously, I was disappointed. But perhaps this was the will of God, I reasoned, so right away I said yes. That's when I first experienced the fruit of obedience. I had great peace and felt assured that as I abandoned myself to God, he would work things out. And after all, training fellow priests was a worthy assignment!

Studies in Montreal and Rome, two and a half years of teaching, more studies in Rome. And then one day a request from the Vatican: could Father Beaudry's order find some theology professors to teach at the seminary in Port-au-Prince?

You can imagine how quickly I responded! And this time, the same superior who had refused me twice said, "Certainly you can go."

But see how wise God is. The only need in Haiti that our order was asked to meet was for seminary professors. Without that advanced degree in theology, I couldn't have come! And my sense of homecoming when I first arrived confirmed that this was the country where God wanted me. Plus, I already spoke French and I learned Creole very quickly. I imagine that if I had been sent to Asia when I first asked to go, I'd still be struggling with Chinese or Japanese!

Seeking the will of God, as Father Beaudry has come to see, gives unity and meaning to every aspect of life.

Prayer is for asking God, "What is your will? What do you want me to do?" You pause and listen, and God's answer comes—like a seed that was there in your soul but needed silence to make it grow into a conviction about which path to take. And once God has shed light on his will for you, then prayer is also for the strength to carry it out. In this way, you continue your prayer throughout the day, in your every activity, as you seek to do God's will.

What do you want me to do now, Lord? Asking that question has led Father Beaudry in directions he didn't expect. Three years after coming to Haiti, he moved into a shanty-town in order to help its residents raise their standard of living. Working with the Legion of Mary—a movement for prayer and evangelism that remains very active in the area—he has helped to improve housing, create jobs, bring in water and electricity, and build a school, medical clinic, church, and workshop.

Everything was built around prayer, he says. So was another project, launched in 1973 at the bishop's request: a prayer center affiliated with the Foyers de Charité, a movement that aims to stir lay Catholics to prayer and social action. Today a group of local men and women help Father Beaudry with the center's main work of giving retreats. So far, thirty-five thousand people have attended.

Here is a version of the first part of a prayer that Father Beaudry wrote as an aid for those who come to the retreat center. Not surprisingly, given how central this theme has become in his own life, the prayer is based on surrender and abandonment to God. *Joyful* surrender, he stresses: "Being happy to be with God, to gaze at him as lovers delight to gaze at one another, to let him do whatever he feels like doing in you—that's prayer."

> **Come. Don't be afraid!**
> **Draw near to God**
> **with small steps of love.**
> **Remove your sandals**
> **and shake off the dust**
> **that makes your heart so heavy.**
>
> **Surrender your being**
> **to the grace of God!**
> **Open yourself up to his life.**
> **Have faith in your faith**
> **to seek out and touch**
> **the Living One who lives in you.**
>
> **To praise God,**
> **breathe in his presence,**

the wind of his Spirit.
Let him enter,
calming your knotted nerves.
Sit down. Relax!

Offer your body
like a bouquet of flowers
full of soul and life:
Your mouth and your eyes,
your nose and your ears,
the touch of your skin.

And then your heart,
your lungs, your brain,
and the blood in your veins.
Gather up your life,
close it off to the outside,
open it up from within....
Go deep down, all the way to your heart,
and find its root:
the spirit plunged in God.

There, remain in peace,
abide in his love,
bathe yourself in his heart.
Listen to his voice,
repeat to him the tender words
that well up in you under his inspiration:

"Father! I am thirsty!"
"I love you, O my Spouse!"
"O come, Spirit of love!"
And then say nothing;
listen to his heart beat
within your own....

Patti Mahfood describes herself as "a throwback to the old-fashioned housewife," with many interests that center around home and family. But working with her husband, who founded Food For The Poor, she travels far beyond home to visit the poorest areas in the Western Hemisphere. Patti moves through these different worlds with gracious serenity. Yet, she says, "I used to be an introvert. I was dragged into Food For The Poor kicking and screaming!"

"I was dragged into this kicking and screaming."

A Change of Heart

"CHANGE THE DIRECTION *in which you are looking for happiness.*" The invitation came from a tall, lean Cistercian monk with a kindly smile and a manner that spoke of humor and intelligence. By the time she heard it, Patti Mahfood was finally ready to accept.

It was a turning point in her spiritual journey, this weekend retreat that Patti and her husband Ferdy were making at a New Hampshire monastery. As Father Thomas Keating explained a way of contemplation that he called Centering Prayer, she sat too spellbound even to take notes. Suddenly a bright light was illuminating some of the painful developments and incidents of the recent past.

I had just returned from grocery shopping and was standing in the kitchen arranging a bowl of apples, bananas, mangoes, and plums. Ferdy walked in and glanced at the mound of fruit.

"Why do you have to buy so many different kinds?" he asked me reproachfully.

"Ferdy," I snapped back, "there are five people in this family and not everybody likes bananas."

I fumed inwardly. *What am I going to do with this crazy husband of mine? He's becoming impossible to live with.* I wasn't the only one who thought so either. Our three teenage children were chafing under Ferdy's dreary attempts to simplify our life. Even old friends were backing away. It hurt me to see them trying to dodge Ferdy. *Probably don't want to be preached at about how they should be helping the poor,* I thought grimly.

Ferdy hadn't always been like this. Not so long ago he had been a normal family man and businessman, with normal interests like fishing. *Why did I ever give him that book?* I had asked myself a hundred times. That's when all the trouble had started—with a Christmas gift I had tucked into his stocking on a whim. Ferdy had had some sort of conversion experience while reading it, and things had gone from bad to worse ever since.

First had come his excitement about prayer, his attendance at prayer meetings and daily Mass. Then, through some missionaries he knew in Jamaica, an interest in the poor. *This will pass,* I kept telling myself. *Give it a year or two.* But it hadn't passed, and now I was alarmed. Ferdy seemed to have lost interest in material things, as if some inner switch had been flipped off. He had drastically simplified his approach to eating and dressing and entertainment, and he was trying to impose his new life-style on all of us. You couldn't reason with him!

By now Ferdy was obsessed with finding ways to help the poor. Lately he had even been talking about living among them. *He's going to want to quit his business and do missionary work,* I worried. *But people like us don't become missionaries! Especially not people like me.*

Unlike Ferdy, I was not feeling close to the Lord or the poor. I was preoccupied with the challenge of adjusting to life in Florida, where we had moved a few years before. After sixteen years in Jamaica, our whole family had found this a difficult transition, one that meant leaving behind many relatives and old friends, and a distinctive way of life. In the process, I also seemed to have said goodbye to the Lord.

With Ferdy working to reform our normal family life and me struggling to maintain it, the tension in our relationship kept building. It was a great relief when Ferdy discovered Centering Prayer: somehow, this made him calmer and more relaxed. He also became less aggressive about converting me, although he did keep trying to introduce me to this new form of prayer that he was so excited about.

Still, my frustration grew day by day, especially after Ferdy launched Food For The Poor. Clearly, we were on diverging paths.

Then one evening a friend of ours, a spiritual writer, visited our home, and he and I had a long talk about Centering Prayer. He explained what it is: a prayer of attentive silence before God that immerses you in the Holy Spirit, puts you in communication with God, and brings peace, wisdom, and healing. "It's like a flower opening and developing in the sun," he told me. "You open your whole self to God, and he gradually touches every part of you. In time, you discover his presence at the very center of your being."

For some reason, the explanation made sense and appealed to me. Maybe I had been too exasperated with Ferdy to really listen to what he had been saying. Or maybe these past five years of seeing the prayer's effects in my husband had prepared me to try it for myself.

That night as soon as our friend left, I went right into my room and prayed for twenty minutes in the way he had described. "Choose a prayer word," he had said. So I made myself comfortable, closed my eyes, and began saying "God" over and over in my mind.

"Change the direction in which you are looking for happiness." Patti had been practicing Centering Prayer for just a short time when she heard Father Keating at that New Hampshire retreat. His lucid explanations of the prayer's effects moved her from simple curiosity to total commitment: "That's when I decided to surrender—to open my mind and heart to wherever God was leading."

I was amazed as I listened to Father Keating unfold his ideas. He blended theology and psychology in a way that I found enlightening and intellectually engaging. *This really speaks to me,* I marveled. I was especially struck by his explanation of how, when we pray, Christ can heal deep inner wounds that have never been addressed. This involves healing what Father Keating called "energy centers"—deep-seated motivating drives for power, esteem, security, and affection.

As Father Keating spoke, I realized that I was trapped in my own personal energy centers. I also had a misguided notion of freedom, I discovered. Freedom does not mean being able to do whatever I want. Father Keating's definition underlined the aspect of surrender: "Freedom is the ability to hear God's call in your life as he wants you to hear it, not as you wish to receive it, and to answer it."

A realization dawned on me: *That's what Ferdy has been trying to do!* Now I understood. Through his sometimes misguided and clumsy attempts to change his life, he had been surrendering to God and responding to his call.

Meanwhile—I suddenly saw it quite clearly—I had been looking for happiness in other directions, in the pursuit of my own goals and interests. Mainly I wanted to live a comfortable life, surrounded by beautiful things. And now that my children were older, I was bound and determined to get that college education I had put aside by getting married in my senior year of high school. Not a bad goal in itself, but now I could see how my fixation with it had blinded me to other possibilities.

Now, with God's help, all that would change, I decided. "I will not fight you any more," I told God. "Lead me wherever you will."

"Change the direction in which you are looking for happiness." Over the years, Patti's crucial decision to seek happiness in God's will rather than her own has led to many changes:

closeness to God, a new sense of freedom, a renewed marriage, and a deep sense of purpose through partnership in Ferdy's work with the poor. It has changed how she looks at many things, Patti maintains. For example, she is still drawn to beauty, she says, but now she can find it in such unlikely places....

I do quite a bit of traveling in connection with Food For The Poor. One day during a visit to Jamaica I walked into a day-care center that had asked for our help. It was a dismal place, badly lit and poorly equipped. Against one dingy wall was a line of rickety cribs. A few battered toys and books were strewn across the floor. I saw nothing beautiful there—not until the young woman who was caring for the children turned away from one of the cribs to greet us.

I've never seen such a beautiful young woman! was my immediate response. She was not well dressed. She had no make-up on, no jewelry, none of the adornments that I had ever associated with beauty. But something was shining through her, something deeper than her physical attractiveness, and I was arrested by it. This isn't the kind of beauty that comes from Nieman Marcus or Saks Fifth Avenue, I realized right away. There's no product on earth that could ever produce such a radiant, transparent look of joy and happiness. *No,* I told myself, *this is the kind of beauty that comes from loving service to others.*

Sometimes now I think back to my early travels with Food For The Poor, when I couldn't detect any beauty whatsoever in all the misery I was seeing. Especially upsetting was my first visit to Haiti. As I walked through the slums with Ferdy, overwhelmed by the sights and smells of abject poverty, I gave myself a pep talk to keep going: *One hour and this will be over with. You'll never have to do it again.*

But I have been back to Haiti since then. Sixteen times. And many more times than that to Jamaica.

Now I can see the beauty that I used to miss—not in poverty itself but in people. I find it in the presence of Christ, humble and hidden, in suffering. I experience it in the simplicity and spontaneity of relationships with the poor. It shines out in the richness of faith and love of God, lived out in the poorest of settings.

And over and over again, I see on the faces of so many of the poor and the people who work with them the same beauty that struck me in that dingy day-care center: the kind that comes from personal surrender into the service of God and others.

Now, that's the kind of beauty I want, too.

For Your Information

EACH OF THE CONTRIBUTORS TO THIS BOOK has some connection to Food For The Poor, an interdenominational, non-profit charitable organization created in 1982 to assist poor people, primarily in the Caribbean and Latin America. It seeks to improve their health and economic, social, and spiritual conditions by channeling funds and services through people who are already working with the poor on-site, usually missionaries and clergy of various denominations.

"We have a simple, hands-on approach," explains founder Ferdinand Mahfood. "We find out from those who are running the local relief efforts what the specific needs are—for sewing machines, rice, bedsheets, or whatever—and then we ask our supporters to help us meet those needs." Today nearly 750,000 men, women, and children participate in Food For The Poor's mission. Over the years their support has translated into shipments of over $250 million worth of food, clothing, medical supplies, and other critically needed goods.

Anyone interested in joining with Food For The Poor to assist people like those whose stories appear in this book may write the organization at:

Food For The Poor
550 SW 12th Avenue #4
Deerfield Beach, Florida 33442

To make a donation or request an information package, call:

(800) 282-POOR

"Every contribution is important, no matter how small. That's the power of combined Christian charity—working together, we can make a difference," Mahfood says. "And in serving the poor, as Matthew 25:40 reveals, we ultimately serve our Lord."